Wo
Plantations Hall
Johnson & Wales University

Who's Afraid of the Dark?

WHO'S AFRAID OF THE DARK?

A Forum of Truth,
Support, and Assurance for
Those Affected by Rape

Edited with an Introduction by

CYNTHIA CAROSELLA

HarperPerennial
A Division of HarperCollins*Publishers*

WHO'S AFRAID OF THE DARK? Copyright © 1995 by Cynthia Carosella. All rights reserved. Printed in the United States of America. No part of this book may be used or reproduced in any manner whatsoever without written permission except in the case of brief quotations embodied in critical articles and reviews. For information address HarperCollins Publishers, Inc., 10 East 53rd Street, New York, NY 10022.

HarperCollins books may be purchased for educational, business, or sales promotional use. For information please write: Special Markets Department, HarperCollins Publishers, Inc., 10 East 53rd Street, New York, NY 10022.

FIRST EDITION

Designed by Nancy Singer

Library of Congress Cataloging-in-Publication Data

Who's afraid of the dark? : a forum of truth, support, and assurance for those affected by rape / edited with an introduction by Cynthia Carosella.
  p. cm.
 ISBN 0-06-095072-2
 1. Rape victims—United States—Interviews. 2. Rape victims—United States—Psychology. 3. Rape—United States—Psychological aspects. I. Carosella, Cynthia, 1963– .
HV6561.W49 1995
362.88'3'0973—dc20   94-39183

---

95 96 97 98 99 ❖/RRD 10 9 8 7 6 5 4 3 2 1

To Chris, in celebration of our
SISTERHOOD

☾

Contents

❨

Acknowledgments

In the past nine years, I have come to appreciate the benefit of having a large family—I can always find support somewhere. I am fortunate too that they are an enlightenned bunch and have done the "right" things to support me. In particular, I want to thank:

My mother, Pat Wahl, for overcoming your fear of flying in order to visit me after I was raped and for all the love you give to me.

My sister Chris, a mentor to many, for always saying yes.

My "bro" Lee, for the happiness you bring her.

My sister Cookie, for understanding what I mean when I say I was guided.

My brother Tony, for the many times you reached out to me over the phone.

My brother Leo, for coming to my graduation.

Debbie, for being a strong woman.

Kristin and Cole, for giving so much love to your aunt.

My brother Matt, the next writer in the family.

Jack, for being on the lookout for information about rape.

My father, Leo Carosella, and Peggy for buying me the Roadrunner.

My grandparents Tony and Edna Carosella, as they celebrate their sixty-fourth year of marriage, for teaching all of us the meaning of giving.

A heartfelt hug goes to my beautiful friend Ruth Walcoff, a constant source of support and dependability, and to your family (my second family)—Brian, Hana, and Sage.

Since this is not the Academy Awards, I'll continue.

My thanks go to:

Jean Spurgeon, for always being home to answer the phone and for your valued friendship.

Donna Giardina, for dropping everything whenever I needed your help and for sharing your home with me.

James Bodinsky, for your generosity and for watching "Seinfeld" with me.

My friends Chris Munro, Margie Cain, Tony Cochrane, Jerry Brockway, Johan Stolpe, and Ellen Mowry, for trying to understand what I was going through and to the rest of the gang for your ideas, concern, and entertainment value: Nancy Lang, Cheryl and Andy Winston, Mern Braun, Chris Tonozzi, Dave Atkins, Jeff Orrey, Eric Van Zura, Guy Schaeffer, and Katherine and Jim Still.

Mary Jo Heindel, my lifelong friend.

Kris and Helen, for being with me when I really needed you.

Jonna Gardner, for your positive thoughts and insight.

Anika Brand, for your enthusiasm.

Judy Allshouse, for letting me be your witness to courage.

Mary Atwater, for thinking of me whenever you came across useful information.

The following reporters and editors for your part in putting me in touch with rape survivors: Mark Obmascek, Claire Martin, Kathleen McCoy, Arlene Shovald, Amy Dressel, Joe Lewandowski, Karen Vigil, Margie Wood, and Ellen Heltzel.

The following for helping me get the book off the ground: Randy Roark, Linnell Juliet, Dr. Deborah Flick, Phillip Gordon, and the Reference Department staff at the Boulder Public Library.

The following people who might not realize why I am mentioning them. Know that your support came at crucial times: Beth Bennett, Mike Breed, Mike Preston, Diane Mayer, Howard Smokler, Dr. Barbara Phillips, Jeanne Duffy-Meyer, Joe MacDonald, and Barbara Johnson.

Anne Byrne, Leigh Allen, and Cassandra Thomas, for your commitment to rape survivors.

My literary agent, Charlotte Raymond, for believing in this project from the beginning.

My editor at HarperCollins, Peternelle van Arsdale, for taking over where I left off and for making this a much better book.

Elizabeth Cross, for seeing what I did not.

Susan Brooks, for teaching me to find the energy I needed to complete the book.

All of the Tyler Smiths in the world.

Zeus, Poncho, Edgar, and Esmerelda, for your many hours of computer companionship.

All of you who have guided me.

Cliff, for bringing more adventure into my life and for your healing touch.

All who shared your stories and confided in me. Even if your words are not here, your spirit and good intentions are.

The contributors, for your bravery, patience, and trust, and for believing that the strength of our generation and the next is dependent upon our ability to uncover the truth.

Introduction

If you are reading this book because you have been raped, welcome.

I write this because five years ago I wandered through a bookstore looking for these words. I knew that I had a need—assurance that the feelings I was having about myself were not unusual. I had been raped more than three years prior and could not rid my mind of the belief that I was "not myself." When I sat down to write a list of the ways in which rape still impacted my life, even I was shocked at my tally of fifty-seven. I then realized that for the first time in my life I had lost my direction and lacked the motivation to find it.

As I had done so many times before, I headed to my favorite bookstore, hoping that I would find some information to help me. I traversed the maze of shelves until I reached the *Women's Studies* section—five bookcases tucked away in a private corner. Books were grouped under the categories of *Career, Health, History, Incest,* and *Marriage/Relationships,* with the remainder of them in *General. Rape* was not a large enough topic to warrant its own heading. I looked through every single book that I thought might have anything to do with rape, becoming painfully paranoid that nearby browsers would deduce my level of desperation. A plethora of literature exists concerning prevention and the immediate aftermath of rape. I did find some good books. Many of them I had already read, but *none of them dealt exclusively with the long-term effects of rape.* It was as if I were looking for chocolate, but carrot sticks were the only thing available. The many statistics and clinical descriptions did not fortify my self-image. That I was part of a group of people that consists of millions of

American women and men did not provide any comfort. What I wanted and needed to know were the emotions and experiences of these people with whom I had so much in common. I wanted a book that would be better than a best friend, a book that understood me, a book that made me feel less alone in the world. I could not believe that somebody had not already realized this need and filled it.

I could clearly envision the intention of such a book: a forum for people who have been raped, whose discussions of the long-term effects of rape would provide the atmosphere of a support group for the reader. I looked back at the shelves and could have sworn that I saw a book with my name on it. It was just a glimpse, but it was enough to convince me that Athena had just dubbed me one of her warriors. I had rediscovered my direction—creating the book I needed.

Rape has always existed, but the opportunity for us to discuss openly its impact on our lives is long overdue. It is time.

Rape Exists Because There Are Rapists, Not Because There Are Victims

One would imagine that an occurrence that is so common in our society would be well understood, but the secrecy, guilt, blame, and myths that cloud the issue of rape prevent it from being so. There are two universal truths about rape: (1) Rape exists solely because of a rapist's motive to control, torment, overpower, abuse, manipulate, hurt, violate. (2) Rape occurs when the rapist(s) is able covertly or overtly to isolate a victim.

Many times we who have been raped fall into the trap of self-blame. We believe that somehow it was our fault. We thereby justify the rapist's actions instead of our own. This is especially true in cases of date rape, whose victims often feel deep regret at not preventing the rape: "If only I had left the party with my friends."

"If only I had not talked to him." "If only I had not had so much to drink."

The only "If only" that is valid is: "If only the rapist had not raped me." We can take responsibility for actions such as trusting a friend, walking to our cars alone, or inviting him back to our place. But we cannot accept the blame for having been raped. It is time to give the blame back to the rapists.

The Disaster Syndrome

According to *Abnormal Psychology and Modern Life*, by R. C. Carson and J. C. Butcher, people who have been exposed to terrifying experiences such as plane crashes, automobile accidents, fires, or sexual assaults tend to respond with what has been described as the "disaster syndrome." The three stages of this syndrome are: (1) the *shock stage*, "in which the victim is stunned, dazed, and apathetic"; (2) the *suggestible stage*, "in which the victim tends to be passive, suggestible, and willing to take directions from rescue workers or others"; and (3) the *recovery stage*, "in which the individual may be tense and apprehensive and show generalized anxiety, but gradually regains psychological equilibrium—*often showing a need to repetitively tell about the catastrophic event*." [my italics]

With no other trauma is the victim so compelled to hide the fact that it has happened. Rape is one of the few crimes that often forces the victim into silence. With a theft, you can tell others and let your anger and worries diffuse out of you. You are not embarrassed to tell others that your car was stolen, and when you get mad about it, you expect everybody else to commiserate. You usually do not doubt that the police will do their best to ensure that justice is sought.

I know of a woman who was in an airplane crash and survived. She was hospitalized just one night for superficial cuts and bruises and managed to walk out with the help of her family and friends. Physically, she was fine. Many differences in her personality, however, gradually became apparent to anyone who knew her, and so everyone understood when she could not return to work full-time. Her business partner took over her duties and did not complain. It was the least that he could do. Her tennis partner understood when it became clear that her friend was no longer interested in competing. Everyone in her life sympathized when she jumped in her car one day and drove over one thousand miles to see her brother and his new daughter. They offered support when she and her husband separated because everybody knows that a traumatic event can be a real stress on a marriage. Now if you replace the first sentence of this paragraph with "I know of a woman who was raped and survived," does it not seem fair that the other ramifications should still follow as true? But rape just does not elicit the same amount of understanding. Because of the stigma associated with rape, we often feel unable to turn to the same support systems that we would normally rely on after any other traumatic event.

A Tool For Recovery

Who's Afraid of the Dark? provides a forum for rape survivors who felt that speaking out would help advance them toward their goals of recovery. It also contains the stories of those who have already reached their goals and wanted to share with you what had worked for them. No two stories are identical, just as no two rapes are identical. Though some aspects of these rapes may be similar, so much of our ability to deal with the aftermath of rape is dependent on factors such as access to a support system, a past history of sexual abuse, personal tactics for problem solving, and resources available.

This book is a tool for recovery; it does not direct recovery.

The intent is to accelerate your process of self-discovery regarding rape's effects by reading about the experiences of women and men who have been raped and are at every stage in the continuum of healing. It will not tell you what is best for you. My hope is that reading these stories will allow you an opportunity to deduce the right pace and path for yourself.

If you ever feel that your experiences have left you all alone in the world, nothing comes as more of a relief than knowing that someone else has lived through something similar and understands. You will experience a sense of confirmation as you read about actions and reactions that are similar to your own. You may feel as if some of these contributors have been able to see directly into *your* mind. You may find an explanation for a feeling that you have been unable to put into words and may be useful to share with those close to you. Sometimes you will agree with all of your heart; of course, you also may come across something that does not ring true for you, or perhaps disturbs you. In this case, just turn the page and move on to something else.

Even though the circumstances of each rape differ, once you have experienced the fear and helplessness of being on the receiving end of sexually expressed violence, you share something with all other survivors. For those of you who have survived the initial crisis stage and have lived for years or even decades with the menacing sense of something amiss, my hope is that this book will help you find the words to describe what you are feeling and the strength to make the necessary changes.

The Effects of Rape Are Far-Ranging, Far-Reaching, Long-Lasting, and Late-Arising

The objective of *Who's Afraid of the Dark?* is to truly grasp the consequences of rape on individual lives. It documents and remembers that which in most cases was never even recognized.

We will never know how many of those who have been raped lost their jobs, ended relationships, experience sexual dysfunctions or addictions or eating disorders or procrastination or loss of direction or loss of hope, etc., all as effects of being raped. I once met a woman who dyed and cut off her hair after she was raped because the rapist had commented on how much he liked her long blonde hair. This had been sixteen years before, and she still could not consider returning to her natural color and letting it grow long. The effects of rape range from subtle to extreme and can be physical and emotional. They range from the man who cannot bear to be spoken to in a certain way by his boss because it reminds him of his rapist's demanding voice, to the woman who cannot bear to lose the protective covering of weight she gained after she was raped.

Rape subjugates our freedom of movement and our freedom of choices. Because we are likely to be extra sensitive to potential dangers, we expend an incredible amount of energy to protect ourselves: watching who is around at all times, deciding which shoes to wear in case the need to run arises, walking to our cars with our keys positioned for use as a weapon, arranging our schedules in order not to be outdoors after dark.

Some of the effects of rape may be entirely unconscious. In fact, many of the contributors to this book blocked out their experiences and emotions during and after the rape to an amazing degree. You will read stories from people who either decided for themselves to repress the rape or were encouraged by others to "put it behind you." In many of these cases, awareness of the effects of rape was not apparent for years or even decades.

Awareness of the Effects of Rape Is the First Step Toward Recovery

One of the first steps you may want to take as a survivor is to start your own list of the ways rape still affects your life. This may be a difficult and emotional experience, so make sure that you provide yourself with uninterrupted time, a support system, and rewards for your accomplishment. Confronting the long-term effects of rape can be painful, but it is also essential; ignored, the size of this unexplored territory will continue to grow. Having the effects before you in black and white provides you with something tangible to work toward in your recovery. It will help you determine what you can live with and what you need to work on.

Because no time limit can be attached to recovery, it is never too late to continue the recovery process. You could be repressing talents and not living at full capacity, always getting by on fumes when you could have a full tank.

Since the time that I wrote down the fifty-seven ways in which rape affected my life on a long-term basis, I have taken steps to eliminate as many of those effects as possible. I know that I will never be the "self" that I was before I was raped, and I realize that some effects will remain with me throughout my lifetime. But at least I have confronted those effects and can make adjustments accordingly. And now with the completion of this book, I have one more effect to cross off the list—loss of ability to complete a project. I relocated the place inside of me where dreams come true. I wish the same for you.

If you are reading this book because you desire a better understanding of how rape has affected someone close to you, then clearly you are someone who is aware that rape affects us all. Because survivors unfortunately often feel compelled to keep this aspect of their lives "in the dark," you may not know how to talk with someone who has gone through this life-altering experience.

You are undoubtedly aware that rape is not only a violation of the body. Many survivors experience a loss of self, as if their souls were penetrated as well. Some feel this loss so strongly that they describe rape as the death of their selves. They feel as if the effects of rape are consuming space within one's body. Keeping this in mind as you read the book will help you understand why giving the standard advice to "put it behind you" is not appropriate. It is comparable to advising someone to leave an arm behind. That does not solve the problem; it only creates another one.

Most survivors agree that the least helpful things to be told— no matter how long ago the rape occurred—are: You "should" have known better or you "should" be recovered by now or you "should" stop living in the past. The reality is that survivors do not *want* to live in the past. When they realize how the past is affecting the present, however, they often need to resolve these issues before moving on.

Probably the best response to a rape survivor is simply to listen to their story without judgment and to ask more than once if there is anything you can do to support their recovery. Each effort that is offered helps to lift the darkness surrounding the effects of rape.

Regardless of your reason for reading this book, you will feel a range of emotions. One of them is likely to be determination to "do something." Don't let that feeling leave you after you've read the last page.

The Stigma of Rape Results from Misconceptions

It was not until I was raped that I realized that the word *rape* is misunderstood. I remember sitting at a café and overhearing a woman tell a friend that she had told her boyfriend to rape her. I wanted to get up and tell her that no one would ever *want* to be raped—to have someone release their violence and need to control by inflicting it on our bodies in a sexual way. Unfortunately, this young woman's ignorance reflects a much wider problem:

Even with what we know after decades of analysis and protests, rape is often not recognized as an essentially violent and malicious act.

An equally harmful misconception is that somehow one can protect oneself from rape. Every day, hundreds discover just how vulnerable we all are. But still, some people secretly believe that rape victims could have prevented it. Survivors are all too often blamed for the crime committed against them—they are called "naive" for having been with a certain person at a certain place at a certain time, or for walking alone, or for not fighting back, or for wearing a skirt that was too short.

Even though a person has a much greater chance of being raped by someone they know than by someone they don't know, the old standard image of rape—a woman is grabbed by an armed lunatic while walking at night—still prevails. A much more likely scenario that results in rape involves a person who is alone with someone they have no reason to distrust. The victim resists, but the rapist insists and uses force or threats instead of a weapon. Just as the country had to have its consciousness raised in the seventies regarding any kind of rape, in the nineties we are still opening minds to date rape and the understanding that the effects of rape are just as devastating whether the rapist was a stranger, a neighbor, or your husband.

Another misconception is that rape victims are "bad" people. But each of us is in danger of being labeled "bad" if a just cause for rape is working in the shed in the backyard, going to a private office for a business meeting, going on a date, sleeping with the window open on a summer night, inviting in a neighbor who has knocked at the door, having lunch with a co-worker, going to the rest room of a restaurant while out to dinner, stopping by a friend's house, or getting some exercise by taking a walk. Rapes have occurred in all of these situations.

Society allows these misconceptions and stereotypes about rape to continue intact, and this in turn creates injustices in our court systems. In rape trials, the female victim is expected to have a picture-perfect past. If she does not fit the "good virgin" mold, the defense attorney goes on the attack. The male victim is assumed to be homosexual. It is no wonder that many people who are raped do not come forward. Coming forward is like volunteering for a public flogging. Just as society is stuck in believing that rapists are strangers, its conception of appropriate sexual behavior is grossly outdated.

Statistics Don't Help

Much media attention has focused on research involving the frequency of rape. I believe that it is time to admit that we will never know the exact number of women and men who have been raped. To those who have been raped, it is not important whether we are part of a group that numbers one in three, one in seven, or one in a thousand. And it is discouraging to witness the energy that is wasted by people who, for whatever reason, desire to discount the frequency of rape. Before I was raped, they probably could have persuaded me of the validity of some of their beliefs. But after I was raped, my beliefs and place in the world changed instantly. To listen to them now is like listening to a woman describe the pain of childbirth without her ever having given birth.

But, speaking of numbers, personally, I do not find it difficult to believe that one in three women have been raped. It was not until I told my friends that I had been raped that many of them told me that they had been as well. When I was raped, I was initiated into a club whose membership is more secretive than any other. Everybody knows a survivor; they just may not know that it happens to be their spouse or friend or co-worker or parent or significant other or child.

Rape dilutes the concentration of potential and harmony in our society by diminishing the quality of life for many of its survivors. I am saddened by the brain power, skills, and talent that are not expressed because of rape. Many young victims do not become what they have dreamt of becoming because the energy to do so often must be diverted toward recovery. Once they reach a point where they are ready to direct some energy for attaining their life's goals, they often have lost the desire to do so or feel that it is too late to start. Those raped later in their lives often lose the momentum that they have built up.

It is time to switch the focus from counting rape survivors to helping them. Society will also benefit—an attempt to counterbalance the damage caused by rapists.

Information Will Lead Us to a Postshame Society

I know that change takes time, but so many voices exist only in the umbrae of the dark, waiting for the safety of the sun to bring them to light. We have few chances to talk about our feelings without making ourselves or those around us uncomfortable. Each survivor deserves to have her or his experience heard and recognized in places other than Take Back the Night marches and bathroom stalls. I like to visualize the day when all rape survivors have their own foundations of support perching them high above the ugliness that guilt, shame, and self-blame can impose.

Thanks to the women's movement, the revelation of discussing the effects of rape is not a *twenty-first*-century phenomenon. The women's movement and the men's movement have helped to expound the principles of victimization and have developed networks of support. But we want a day when those who have been raped are treated like victims of any other crime—no stigma attached. It is time to take the next step.

Information is power: power to recover, power to teach, power to change. One of the best ways to learn about an issue is to study its effects. For those of us who are willing to face the possible discomfort of exposing our secrets, we have the information that will lead us to a postshame society. As more and more voices are heard, the network grows and we start to feel less lonely. It is the key to bringing light to the darkness that we all have known. I feel some hope in the winds of change that have been blowing lately, and I invest my hope into the pages of this book.

One year ago, I returned to my favorite bookstore to find that the *Women's Studies* section had been moved. It is now twelve bookshelves big and is centrally located with large reading chairs that encourage daylong visits. The shelf signs now include *Eating Behaviors, Addictions/Recovery, Incest/Child Abuse, Family Therapy, Grieving/Loss, Gender Studies, Marriage/Relationship, Sexuality, Gay & Lesbian Studies, Journal Writing,* and *Sexual Assault/Domestic Violence. Men's Studies* was also located in this area. I had to say "excuse me" a number of times in order to make my way past all of the women and men who were congregating there. Instead of feeling paranoid as before, I joined in the solidarity of the section, enjoying the sense of self-help in the air. After all, isn't self-improvement what life is all about?

As I made my way to *Sexual Assault/Domestic Violence,* I half-hoped that I would find a book entitled *The Long-term Effects of Rape as Expressed by Those Who Have Been Raped.* That would get me off the hook. I would become resolved to the idea that someone else had beat me to the punch line. I saw some new titles and perused their pages for something about long-term effects. The other half of me, which had become dedicated to seeing this book project to an end, became excited as I realized that there was still not a book that dealt exclusively with the long-term effects of rape. My adrenaline flowed as I realized that I had to do it. I had to make the book materialize not only for myself but also for the many who entrusted me with their thoughts, and for all of the others who like myself have stood looking at the bookshelves trying to find it.

About This Collection

This collection contains the words of people who wanted to have their trauma recognized and hope to help others at the same time. Those interested in contributing their stories contacted me after reading articles about this project in newspapers throughout the United States. Respondents were asked only the following question: How are you and your life different now than before you were raped? I did not use a specific definition of rape nor did I ask for a description of the rape(s). For some survivors, it was important to include details about the rape(s) in order to draw correlations between it and its effects or to communicate the horror of the violence that takes place in our society. I have encapsulated explicit details within rule lines. If you find it too disturbing to read the specifics of what these people were able to withstand, please skip over these sections and read on.

This collection does not include the stories of female and male incest survivors for two reasons. First, while rape and incest survivors share many common issues and concerns, the recovery process can be quite different. And second, so many wonderful resources already exist which can better tackle the very complex issue of incest and childhood sexual abuse. However, some contributors to this volume have experienced both incestuous and nonincestuous rape and have chosen to write about how this multiple violation has affected their lives.

The pieces are arranged chronologically, from the most recent rapes to the less recent. Chapter Two and Chapter Thirty were written by men who were raped. Too many still are surprised that this crime occurs. As with female rape, male rape exists solely because of the rapist's motive to control and violate. And male rape occurs when the rapist is able to isolate a victim.

While this forum was designed to provide confidentiality, some of the contributors chose to use their names. Thus, all names and locations published in this book are real. If a respondent did not want to use her/his name, I felt it better to use no name at all than to simulate an identity through the use of a pseudonym. While reading a story written by "this woman" may seem impersonal, it is an unfortunate reminder that those who have been raped often only feel comfortable with speaking out when anonymity is guaranteed. The contributors' choice is a reflection of my belief that those who are raped have the right to decide if their identities should be made public. Until society has a better understanding of rape, no blanket law regarding the use of victims' names will be acceptable to all. Therefore, I believe the victims' rights should continue to override those of the public's right to know. Regardless of their decisions on name usage, all of these contributors are pioneers in eliminating the stigma of the rape victim. Their stories represent a spectrum of experiences from people of all walks of life—young, old, poor, wealthy, diverse races and religions. Some didn't report the crime, and others didn't realize that it was rape at the time. Some were raped by an acquaintance, others by spouses, and some were too young to give the crime a name. I am privileged to have had the opportunity to compile the words of so many wise people. I am confident that you will admire the bravery that they have exhibited in tapping into private thoughts.

1

Do I Get Summer This Year?

)(

Megan Ann was raped almost four years ago at the age of thirty-four by the mechanic who worked on her car. Recognizing symptoms of shock immediately afterward, she made a call to a friend. "I think I've been raped. Have I?" Soon after, she wrote of the philosophical and moral right to commit suicide and presented it with furious conviction to friends. They grew concerned, and a hospital stay was recommended. She followed their advice, thinking she might at least get some rest. Two days were enough for her to know that "cracked lives don't get fixed in psychiatric hospitals. The only place to go was back . . . back into the frightening world to feel and work and wait for the sun to shine again."

June twenty-first, summer begins. June twenty-fifth, winter sets in unexpectedly—a colder, harsher season than I remember. Other people wear shorts and sunglasses, rubbing on sunscreen and commenting on the heat. I am loosely wrapped in bulky, dark clothing that offers no protection from the icy winds of bitter thoughts. Doesn't everyone feel the chill? Aren't you afraid, looking at the dim sun in bleak skies?

I cautiously check faces in the grocery store. Not one reflects the insistent threats I feel. Fear radiates and bounces off of objects and people. Time to hurry home and lock the door against . . . ?

Fear with its many faces—bottomed-out self-esteem, hatred and repugnance for the body, lack of attention to life, to name a few. These are burdensome companions when they define each and every bit of life. Even sleep and dreams become seared by the strange experience of emotional volcanoes erupting below the deep frozen ice of fear.

This is my legacy as the survivor of rape.

How does it feel to live in such a world?

Every moment is heightened by panic. I came to believe in the reality of the chemical barrage of fear-driven adrenaline in my body. "Yes, the world and all in it, including myself, are dangerous." So, don't shower; I'll be alone with "the body." Don't dress up or look my best; I'll only attract danger. Anything that benefited my physical self became suspect and an emotional trial I couldn't face.

. . . Sadness, oh, my poor body. So hurt and confused, so female and spoiled . . .

Most nights I fell asleep in my clothes on the couch, teeth unbrushed, face unwashed, exhaustion that never matched the events of my day.

Talking softly, mumbling, stuttering and avoiding eye contact are other good ways to hide. I know—I used them for over two years. As a former actress and dancer, it was particularly painful to lose the ability to present myself well. My ease with words had always been with me and I was actually stuttering! It seemed worse when I tried to talk about myself, my heart, my inner world.

. . . Fear of exposure, of ridicule. Rejection. A damaged person cannot live in the same world with others. They are not fit . . .

It is horrible to look into a friend's face and feel shame. Using my support system was very difficult. How could I ask for nurturing when I had so little to give? When I felt I was some lone Arctic native, shrouded in hides and fur?

Wearing the appropriate work face was impossible. I stepped off the corporate management track; I didn't believe I could do what I already *was* doing, so I disappeared into a small hub office, downplayed my abilities and created a safe haven of invisibility. Now everyone believes my timid facade.

Intimate relationships have eluded me. Naturally I can come up with many reasons, but fear is the base. Fear of being seen, of being known, as if I carry some brand on my pelvis that shrieks "RAPED" or "NO GOOD." Perhaps I expect a man to pale and stumble out as soon as possible, horrified by my ugly, frozen-slab-of-meat body.

Looking out at other women's lives, I saw only joy and fulfillment. Why them? Even the eighteen-year-old checkout girl appeared to *love* her life. Have I forsaken life or has it forsaken me? Such questions open a fissure in the ice, and pain flows forth. I must not be as deserving as they are. That's why it happened. God is showing me my true worth.

GOD OF THE PAST laughs at me and the ice caps tremble. I am left bereft in the snow and wind with a haunting echo biting my bones. "You deserve every moment of terror and sorrow. Feed me with your pain; it is the offering I demand."

I truly believed this for a long time. I have broken with my personal cult; I understand that I never really heard the voice of God, only my own despair, speaking in a booming tone to hide shaking hands. Rape does that to a person, makes you want to believe in SOMETHING SOLID. Unfortunately, self-hate is usually closest at hand and matches the general emotional tone of the barren postrape world. (Ah! Another clue that self-destruction is the way. . . .)

You might think such a crazy life would be exciting. It's actually quite boring. Some days drag on and life itself becomes another chore. I walk through those days in the fog of a slave, waiting for the drudgery to end. Some evenings are reserved for gnawing that day's bones of jealousy and abandonment.

And then there are all the other days. I forced myself to commit to a weekly women's group and found sympathetic ears that never turned from me in boredom. I found the environment I needed to heal without overwhelming my family and friends. Because they consistently reflected me as being a lovable woman I have become convinced that I AM worthwhile. I took walks and consciously tried to feel the earth, to connect with my body in everyday activities. I slowly moved from the couch to my own bed. Daily self-care became easier as I invested in myself. A male friend gave me the opportunity to take the Model Mugging self-defense course, and I gained the freedom of confidence. My attempts at dating haven't put me beyond anxiety, but I understand I am different from what I was and it's going to take time to feel comfortable again. My standards for relationships are higher because I value myself so much more; that's probably part of why they seem so much harder to find!

Some inner will to survive kept me plodding through the ice storms that beat upon me, and I began to notice my world looking brighter. First, a reflection on my boots and slowly raising my head, the sun. I made room for the experience of being in the present, my own present, a place and time "he" will never find because "he" is trapped in the iceberg.

My life is becoming a life I want to live, because I know it is *mine*.

Yet, I wistfully look back and wish it had all been different: that the beautiful month of June was never stained, that I never felt soiled and degraded, that these years and all their possibilities weren't gone forever, that I could have read my story in a book instead of living it.

I will always wonder who I'd be if another person hadn't rearranged the seasons and with unthinking violence taken away my summer.

2

One Trucker's Blues

❡

WALK WITH ME. WALK WITH ALL OF US. THERE NO LONGER IS THAT NEED FOR ISOLATION AND LONELINESS.

Stephen Grubman-Black

I am not afraid anymore of people knowing what has happened to me. I am telling my story in this book for other people who have been raped, to encourage them to get help. Don't let it drag on. Whoever wants to read this book can know my name—Randy Reed Walker. I want to be here when this book is published, but I don't know if I will be. I have AIDS. I am a reminder that people who are raped have to deal not only with the effects of the violent act itself, but also with the fear that the rapists gave them HIV. I have nothing to lose. I have already hit the bottom; I am climbing back up.

In my sixteen years as a truck driver, I went all throughout the forty-eight contiguous states. I learned a lot. I learned about history—more than I ever did before I dropped out of school. I learned about people's feelings. I learned how to respect human beings regardless of whether I liked them or not. I learned how to be polite and just cut off a person and go someplace else instead of getting into a big heated discussion or argument or fight.

Nothing that I learned could have prepared me for the morning of November 7, 1989. I was raped. It happened in Manassas, a small town in the woods of Virginia. Way back in the woods, there is a pull-off road where drivers can sleep. After your truck gets loaded, you pull off and get yourself some snooze before you get ready to do your thing. The morning that this happened to me, I had driven all day and half of the night, so I pulled over onto this dirt cul-de-sac and went to sleep.

When I got up that morning, two men walked up to me and one of them held a gun to the side of my head. He said, "What kind of money you got?" I said, "Man, I ain't got no money." I had fifteen dollars and a credit card that could only buy diesel. When they found the fifteen bucks and no other credit cards, one of them told me that I'd have to pay in another way.

They told me to drop my pants. I told them that they were going to have to kill me first. I know about guns and I had a gun in the cab of the truck, but there was no way that I could get to it. I heard him pull the hammer back, and I thought that I was going to die . . . so I let both of these men rape me.

I did not see what they looked like. All I heard was the car door slamming and I did not even turn my head to see what the car looked like. The first thing I thought was that I was not going to tell anybody. I knew that I had to be checked for venereal diseases though. I knew that. And later, I had to consider that I was at risk for getting AIDS.

I had the load on, so I started driving. I did NOT know what to do. I went to a liquor store, got back in my truck which had a sleeper, closed the curtain and just stayed back there and drank. Finally, I knew that I had to contact somebody or else the state police were going to be looking for me.

I called my boss. He was a deputy sheriff, but he owned the company. He did not know how to handle it. He wanted to know if I could complete my load. I said that there was no way that I could drive. I told him that I would endanger people on the highway. I told him that not only had I been drinking but that my mind was in no shape to be out on the highway. He told me to talk to his secretary. I told her that I was tired of goofing around, that they needed to get me home. I knew that they could get a driver to fly in and take over the load and get me home. My wife had called and told my boss to get me home.

While I was waiting, I went to a nearby hospital to be checked out. Everyone's question was the same: *You* were raped? Two more days passed until my boss finally agreed to fly me home.

My wife was really nice to me . . . the first couple of days. She had scheduled me to meet a counselor at the Austin rape center. I met with her and everything was fine. I was trying to deal with it. I went forward and did the whole bit, but our life was not the same. Before the rape, my wife and I used to pinch each other on the butt, kidding around and stuff. When I got back, she did that and I told her never to touch me there again—NEVER. That hurt her. The fun and games were out. Joking around and wrestling and giggling and touch and fun—I couldn't do it after I was raped.

My wife kept telling me that I had to get strong so that I could go back to work. She worked, but I made better money than she did. Thirty days later I was back out on the road. My counselor told me I was not ready. I told her I had to go. I did file a claim through workman's compensation, and this took a long time. A *male* was raped? They did not believe it. They asked me if I would take a lie detector test. I said that I would not. I said that I had been subjected to questioning by a police detective and that a doctor had checked me over. The doctor confirmed that I had been raped.

When I went back on the road, my first load was to New York City. No problem. Out of New York City, I was sent right back to Manassas, Virginia, to the exact same place that I had been raped. My boss asked me how I felt about going there. I told him that I knew I'd have to go back there at some point if I worked for him. I went back there seven times. The only time that my company was allowed to load or unload was between two and six in the morning. So every time that I got to a dock, it was right during the same damn time that I was raped.

I had talked to a woman counselor in Austin because I did not want to talk to a man. I did not want to look at a man and tell him that I had been raped. She was really good with me. She got me across the country a few times. Late in the evening—I might have driven five or six hundred miles—I would call her at home asking her to get me another hundred miles. Then when I knew that I had to go to this place in Manassas, I would talk to her constantly. She helped me get there and get out without my going goofy, without turning down the load and losing my job.

For a while after the rape, I got into drinking really heavily. Now I did not drink when I was driving, but I was still half-lit in the morning when I got up to drive that truck again. I would barely eat anything and drive seven hundred miles. Then I'd hit a bar. If I didn't like the bar, I'd hit a liquor store and I would just drink by myself. By myself . . . all night long . . . in the sleeper. I'd talk to myself and cry.

My wife would not touch me. She would not even sleep with me. We had sex one time after I was raped and we used a condom. Naturally I was scared. I did not feel right and she did not feel right. I went through this for almost two years with her. Then the company that I was with went owner-operated, so I lost my job. My wife told me to get out. I took a hundred dollars, plane fare, and four boxes, and I left.

Now I live with my seventy-two-year-old mother, who has only a very small pension and Social Security. She can't afford to have me. Her maximum income is nine hundred dollars a month. The rent is three-fifty. She has to give me money for gas. I'm trying to quit smoking because that's so expensive and then there is food and utilities.

Fifteen months ago, I started getting really sick. I had no energy and was coughing and vomiting constantly. I wasn't working, so I had no money. I went down to a clinic and they took blood. Two weeks later, they said that I was HIV positive.

I contacted my wife and told her. She did not want to believe it, so I contacted her father. We had been really good friends. He had a great deal of respect for me and he still does. He finally got her to take a test. Well, she was negative. I contacted the woman that I had known prior to my wife and I told her. She was negative. So I know in my heart that I got this through the rape.

I wanted to help other men who had been raped. That is why I got involved with a rape crisis center. I know sometimes that male victims don't like talking to a woman, even though it was easier for me to talk to one first. I figured that I could help somebody and direct them into getting help. But when I got my first call, I did everything wrong. Everything that they taught me— look in the book and give them referrals—I did not do. I tucked this man under my wing like a mother with her child. I felt that person's pain so strongly that I told myself that I had to be there for that person. The director of the rape crisis center could see that this man's rape was tearing me apart and that I could not handle it in a proper way. I understood and resigned.

One bright spot from all of this was that I met "Brown Eyes." She was a volunteer for the rape crisis hot line also. We were such close friends, especially for a male and female. We did not have to worry about one of us trying to attract the other one. We did everything together and had a good time even if we weren't doing anything in particular. She was my only friend and I could tell her anything.

Brown Eyes had been sexually abused by her brother for fifteen years. She was under psychiatric care, and they gave her a lot of narcotics—lithium, Xanax, quite a few others. Two days before her twenty-sixth birthday, she died from an overdose. She had it planned because she had tucked away a bunch of pills. She used to laugh about the fact that she just had to call in and get her medication without seeing her psychiatrist. She could even get it refilled more frequently than prescribed and he would not ask her why. She left a four-year-old son.

I have seen a lot of death. I grew up in the drug era. I saw people die from overdoses. I have seen people die in accidents out on the road. After Brown Eyes's death, everything that had happened to me built up on me. I just reached the point where I said, "I want to go. I'm tired of this." That is when I decided that it was time to check out.

Well, I tried, but it didn't work, and I'm not doing it again. I put my mother through hell. I slit my wrist the way that everybody says to do it. I was lying in a warm bath, and I passed out. My mother got the blood to stop flowing and she kept an eye on me. When I woke up, I thought that I was dreaming. I thought that I was dead. I pinched myself and I lay there until my mother walked up. She said, "You've got to get yourself some help. Now!" Then I knew that it wasn't a dream. I honestly thought that when I did this that I'd be gone. When I woke up and I was in the real world again, I said, "Randy, you're an ass." I knew that since I survived I was supposed to be here.

I know that I am not the only truck driver who has been raped. There are so many men out there who are subjected to rape. If men have been out there long enough, they have encountered it in hotel rooms, places where they stop off for coffee, or rest areas. Truckers sleep on city streets in the Bronx, Manhattan, downtown Detroit, Chicago. We know that muggings happen, and we hope that we will live through it when it does. But a man never thinks that he will get raped!

I want to blame all of this on somebody, but I can't. I want to take my anger out on somebody. I have tried other methods like running and karate, but I get really tired and sick. If I overexert myself, I get sick. Every time I get a little cough, I get scared and think that this is it.

I am under medication right now—a mild antidepressant that is not addictive. My doctor wanted to give me an addictive one, but I said that I did not want it. What I have helps to calm me down, but I still wake up with very bad nightmares every once in a while.

I have my good days and I have my bad days. Now I take AZT. I try to keep my sense of humor. I always thought that I had a good sense of humor. I'm a pretty good gabber and I like to shoot the bull. I like to talk to people. I like to go out and have fun. Since I was raped, I have had little social contact. I would love to meet people. It'd be nice to have some friends to goof around with, but I feel that AIDS prevents me from doing this. My psychologist suggested I join an AIDS support group. In the first one I tried, I was the only one who was not homosexual—not that there is anything wrong with that. I just felt like I didn't belong. In the group I'm in now, one person got it from a blood transfusion and another was a paramedic who got it from treating someone who had it.

There are not too many women out there, probably none, who would want to have a relationship with me. Even if a woman said that she could handle this, I cannot fulfill the needs that she would have and she cannot fulfill the needs that I have. I don't want to put that person through the pain that I am going to go through. I'd rather go through it on my own. But now I am going to contradict myself because I would love to have somebody to love me and understand me and hold my hand and kiss me. I know that I can be caressed, but I can never make love again, and I can't have children.

I did a lot of things that weren't right in my younger years, but I have tried to be a good person. I know in my heart that I don't deserve this. I don't like it, and there is nothing that I can do about it. It hurts. It tears me up, but I'll do anything I can to help.

I am grateful that my experience can go into this book. I was ashamed that I was a man who had been raped. I know that I can never ever forget this, but I have to learn how to deal with it. I have to learn how to go forward. I have to stop letting the past drag that chain behind me. I have to do it, otherwise I am going to destroy myself and the people around me. My mother tries to be supportive, but I know in her mind that she figures she is too old for this. I had been on my own since I was sixteen years old. I made good money when I was driving a truck. I was very secure. I was saving up for a home. I lost it all.

They say that "life is a bitch and then you die." I definitely believe that, but I am trying to make it better. Today I cannot believe that I am involved with a book about rape. There is no way that I thought that this could happen to me. I always thought that I would die in a truck going off a cliff somewhere. I could not imagine that my whole life would completely change from being a happily married truck driver to dealing with rape and AIDS. If I can talk to another man and help, I would love to do it. A lot of men who have been raped are probably wondering if they should get help. They have hidden it. They are married and have nice children and don't want to tell their wives. They don't want to tell anybody. They just go on. Today more women talk about their experiences of having been raped. Now *men* have to do it as well.

Nine months ago, my doctors told me that I would not live until the holidays. Here it is, February, and I am still here. Those doctors do not realize that they are dealing with an ornery, red-headed Swede. When they first told me this, I accepted it. But it did not take me long to set out to prove them wrong. Part of my attitude adjustment came from taking part in the From All Walks of Life AIDS march. It was incredible to be surrounded by so many people who understand how I feel. We were all singing and waving banners. This was the first time since knowing that I have AIDS that I have felt like there is hope. I now know the strong connection between how my mind feels and how my body feels. I really take care of myself now. In fact I'm doing much better than I was when those doctors gave me my death sentence. I hung my banner from the march up on the wall. Now my goal is to live, so that I can be singing right along with everyone else when the march happens again this year.

3

Introspection

❨

I WANT HER FEAR TO HAVE LASTED
JUST AS LONG AS RAPE LASTED SO
THAT THE FEAR COULD HAVE BEEN
CONTAINED . . . THE FEAR DID NOT
STOP BUT PERMEATED EVERY-
WHERE.

The Woman Warrior
Maxine Hong Kingston

When Anne Elizabeth initially attempted to analyze how rape had changed her, she was confused and frustrated; nothing came to mind. After some thought, she realized that because she was only fourteen when the rape occurred, which was eight years ago, the incident had not *changed* her as much as it had *formed* her. In almost every aspect of her personality she can still recognize influences of the rape.

I am an extremely private, even secretive person now. This I can say was an immediate result of the rape, or an actual change in my nature. Most noticeable was that I no longer wanted to go to school. Grades seven through twelve were all in the same building. I was not only ashamed and afraid to see him (he was an eighteen-year-old in the twelfth grade) but also realized that others had found out that we were "together," and I was angry and embarrassed about what they thought they knew—that I had willingly been with him.

The night I was raped, I had attended a party with two of my girlfriends. They had left angry with me because they thought I had decided to sleep with this person. They had already planned to spend the night at my house and had arrived there an hour before me. When I came in crying, my friends were accusatory. I remember saying, "Please listen! You guys don't understand." The first thing one of them said before proceeding to lecture me was, "We just understand that you are a slut and no one will care why." My parents slept through the whole scene. I didn't say another thing to anyone about it for three years.

I spent those teenage years feeling alone and alienated. I missed an average of fifty school days each year. My parents couldn't figure out what in the world was wrong with me. Sometimes I just couldn't bear to see people; sometimes it was that I was exhausted from staying up all night to avoid the nightmares; sometimes I was just plain sick from the various eating disorders I had developed. I was extremely suicidal as I entered high school—the longer I held it in, the more problems I developed and the more I just felt suicide would be the only way to end them. I finally told my best friend about the rape when I was seventeen. Many of the suicidal feelings ended. We decided that the most important thing would be for me to get away from my town and all of the memories. Whenever possible, we went on road trips or vacations. Eventually I decided to go to college in another part of the country.

Spending so much time alone has made me an extremely introspective person. As a young teen, there was a large communication gap between my friends and me because I thought about life, death, and the tendencies and injustices of the world, while they thought about the big game or cute boys. This also led to my development of a strong faith in God—not only because I often felt it was the only place to turn but also because there were so many days that were so low that I don't know how else I could have pulled through.

I learned to separate things that are spiritual or emotional from things that are physical—a difference like black and white. This has manifested itself in various ways. First, I decided how much material objects actually mean in my life. I concluded that anything that broke or was taken could be replaced.

Another, more direct separation was my sexuality. The rape had been my first sexual experience, and, perhaps needless to say, it shattered every "Cinderella" dream I had ever held. It was almost a necessity to make emotions and sex two distinctly unconnected things. I once wrote in a poem that if I had tried to connect them it would mean that physical "closeness was based in hatred, tearing confusion and destruction of all personal claims to choice." Until recently, this separation led me to be promiscuous. In a sense, noncommittal sex helped me to reinforce the idea that anything physical need not affect me emotionally. I have since changed this attitude and allowed myself to learn what it means to make love.

The comment that was forever cemented in my mind on the evening of the rape was "Trust me." That night, the most honest trust was violated by him in raping me, by my friends who would not listen, and by a society that only acknowledged rape as being committed by people who appeared to be "lowlifes" and strangers. I have learned to trust in myself above all else and to be in control of situations both physically and emotionally. This, of course, has positive and negative ramifications. I have no sense of humor over a boyfriend jokingly wrestling me to the ground, but at least I am not stuck in situations that leave me physically vulnerable. I am often criticized for seeming apathetic about many things, but I have kept myself from feeling emotionally drained by not allowing myself to become upset about things that I know won't matter in five years.

I have tried to be as objective as possible in viewing the world. As my experience taught me, things are not always as they appear. As upsetting as this has been, it has also led to a sense of personal empowerment. Although I am in no way careless about preventing this from ever again happening, I am confident that if I survived that rape at such an unsure point in my life, I can survive anything. I now fully believe in the concept "that which does not kill us makes us stronger"—at least eventually.

Ironically, where I initially felt the need to be secretive in order to deal with the rape, I now am learning that speaking out is a necessary step to help with my healing. Once I have dealt with those who are close to me, I would like to begin working with elementary and junior high education on this issue. It has definitely influenced my career choice—law. There needs to be changes in all levels of society's consciousness—not only in prevention but also in punishment and just accountability. It is a rare day that I do not further analyze or feel a degree of pain from that one hour of my life eight years ago. Each day, though, I realize that some aspect of the experience, which at one time meant only pain, can now work in moving me toward a positive future. It has taken over eight years to begin this transformation. This is where I have learned to be patient and to persevere.

After writing the above, Anne Elizabeth decided to tell her family about the rape. Their support and relief in knowing the cause of her pain convinced her to go into therapy. Her thoughts on learning to control the effects:

There is no such thing as "getting over it." I waited for many years for the day when the rape would not bother me. The feeling that this day would never come gave me a sense of hopelessness; I had tried everything imaginable to shut out the pain, only to realize that denying the hurt of the experience allowed it to upset other areas of my life. The memories are painful. They should be.

I will never forget that I was raped, and it will never be less than an extremely hurtful experience. I will never get over it, but I don't have to be controlled by it. Rape is like the blob, and the pain of it will seep into every day, every relationship, and every aspect of life if it is not contained. The rape, or some effect of it, formerly consumed my whole existence. But I do not have to "forget it" in order to control it. I no longer have to figure out how to fit my life into the rape and into a constant sense of being victimized. Instead, I consider how this experience and the unique knowledge that accompanies it can fit into my life.

4

Romeo's Antithesis

❛

This woman found it very odd that someone had requested to know how she felt about date rape because she had been "slammed so many times in the past eight years for not getting over it." She decided to write when she realized that having her story in a book would validate its importance outside of her own life. She is twenty-five.

When I was nineteen, I explained the circumstances of my rape to a man who I was dating. This man commented that since I had slept with the rapist once, he could see how the rapist might have been allowed certain subsequent rights to my body. Swell. I no longer date this man or any man like him. Because of the rape, I view men through a thick filter that allows me to see the callous bitter parts of their personalities even as I see things that I love.

There are certain facts concerning the rape that I feel need to be explained. I was raped when I was only seventeen by a boy one year older than me with whom I was friends: a boy who took me to the prom, a boy I had a desperate crush on, a boy I had willingly slept with once, a boy who felt that he was entitled to take anything he pleased.

On the night I was raped, we had seen Shakespeare's *Romeo and Juliet*: very romantic, spirited, full of life, and very, very tragic. I can remember every single character in that play even though I don't have a program. Afterward we went to a girlfriend's apartment, the three of us, and smoked pot and perhaps drank some beer, mightily pleased that we were doing something very adult and forbidden. I fell asleep (or did I pass out? Does it matter?) in the double bed, my girlfriend on one side and he on the other. Perhaps she was asleep, perhaps she thought my protests were unreal, maybe she did not hear. In any case, she made no move to help me. Later she discounted my perception of the situation and told me I wanted it. Mainly I remember pain (I bled for many days after), suffocation (I was tangled in my clothes), and fear of being pregnant. Part of me watched and made narrative comments: "His hand is on your breast" and "You cannot move." (Later a psychologist called my narration dissociation.) He got me up, got me dressed, and took me home. I remember clinging to the door on the passenger's side with that voice in my head saying, You will be home soon, repeated over and over.

That girlfriend was the first person I told; it took me a long time ever to tell anyone else—four years to tell my mother, who was relieved to know my problems with men were not all her fault. It was six years before any counseling. I told each of three subsequent boyfriends, and I gave sketchy details to a number of girlfriends and acquaintances. Sometimes talking makes me feel better—I gain retroactive power.

I am afraid of the dark. I carry a flashlight to my car. I turn all hall lights on before entering dark rooms. Even though I knew my assailant, I fear anonymous attack. When I walk to my car at night, I always hold my keys with the sharp end between my fingers and the base securely in my palm. (Self-defense tapes will say that the key can be used to poke out an eye.) I heard a story about a woman who approached her car at night and was grabbed from underneath the vehicle, both her legs broken from the violence before she was raped. (Was she killed? I can't remember.) I check under the car, I check the backseat, I get in quickly and lock the doors, I turn on the lights, I check the backseat again and I double-check the locks. I sometimes have bizarre thoughts that I will find someone dead in my house, in the closet or in the tub. I asked my fiancé if he thinks such things. He says no. Perhaps only women think these things; maybe it is only me. Sometimes as I approach my car with my little key weapon, I try to imagine what good it would do me against a man with a gun, or a big man, or one with a knife. I see myself saying, "Hold still while I poke you in the eye with this thing."

I can't tolerate drugs or alcohol or the people who do them. Everyone tells me it wasn't my fault, but I know one thing for certain: If I had been sober, I would not have been raped. How can I know this? Sobriety is the only power I have. If you take it away, it means it could happen again. If you say I had no control, that it was all him, then afterward all I am left with is no control.

Perhaps it is only an imagined control, but it is all I have and it helps me go on.

Two years later he looked up my phone number and called me. That was frightening. He said he was sorry and asked me to go out with him again. I called him every rude name I ever learned. I told him to leave me alone and never to talk to me again. At the beginning of the call, he said he was going into the military. I hope he was in Panama or the Persian Gulf, and I hope he died in some pitiful, painful, cowardly way. After that call, I cried and shook with disbelief and horror. I blockaded the door. I was afraid he was down the street at a pay phone and knew my address. Later when my boyfriend at the time came home, I told him about the call, and he said, "Interesting." See how little he understood? For nearly two years after that, I would not answer my own phone: I let the machine take all calls. Now I don't have my name listed in the phone book. My mother does not give out my number. I only give my number to close friends and employers. Still when I pick up the phone and the other party hangs up, I worry it is him, or someone worse, waiting to see if I am home. Alone.

I am afraid to be alone. An unfortunate contradiction is that I like to be alone, or at least I think I do. This is the one fear that seems to be getting worse over time. At this time I am hardly ever alone in the literal sense of the word. I don't like to be in my home alone or to drive by myself or to walk alone. I get a sort of pseudo-aloneness in cafés or parks, where I can build a cocoon of space around myself and not be with others and not be alone. There is safety in numbers.

I don't like people to touch me. The exceptions are my fiancé's touch and that of my massage therapist, who works in a professional and somewhat distant manner. People who want to hug me (friends, relatives, even my mother) make my stomach turn with their overtures. I know this touching is affection yet it sickens me. Waitresses or professional peers who touch me, even in the most casual manner, make my skin crawl. I like to have space between myself and others.

The more that I write, the more that I can think of to say. I don't particularly care for dogs, yet I like to live with them for safety. I like to have men record my answering machine message so that nobody thinks I might be a woman living alone. I have had endless stomach and female problems since the rape, including the genital warts he gave me. I have had to explain this to each man I have considered sleeping with because this disease may remain in remission for up to ten years. I have no desire to dress in a sexy manner in public. Men who look at me with lasciviousness make me uncomfortable. I prefer to be a little heavy (or to feel I am a little heavy) to detract attention from myself. I have a paranoia about the vehicle he owned and still suspiciously notice that type of vehicle on the street (even though it happened eight years ago and he has undoubtedly changed cars). I am angry that a man who I despise could impact my life every day, forever.

5

No Surefire Answers

❦

Rebecca hopes that society soon realizes a person needs more than just a few months to recover from rape. After eight years, she still feels its effects. A supportive family and friends can ease the burden, but she believes rape survivors need opportunities where they can speak out.

How is my life different since I was raped? I ask you how isn't it? When I was raped, I was seventeen years old, a recent high school graduate, a teenager on top of the world. Then my world was shattered. A close friend and employee of my father entrapped me and watched as a friend of his raped me. I was afraid to tell people for two reasons: (1) I thought that some would not believe me; (2) I thought that others would take matters into their own hands. The friends I did tell wanted to hurt both of them. I had to deal with their anger in addition to my own emotions.

Initially, I was so lost and confused that I did not believe I was raped. My friends and I recognized that what had happened was wrong, but we did not know at the time that someone could be raped by a friend. It was not until I attended a rape presentation in college that I learned of the term date rape. I did not need the violation to be labeled, however, to realize that my life had become ruled by fear, pain, anger, and self-doubt.

The fear that permeated all aspects of my life was very difficult to control. I was raised on a ranch where fear was considered to be a weakness. After the rape, I was afraid to be alone; yet, I was afraid to be with people. All my life, I had male friends and had worked around men. After the rape, men changed from friends to potential rapists. I found it difficult to see men as individuals. My fear of them included a fear of sex. I was a virgin when I was raped, and it had been important to me to be a virgin when I got married. Eventually I tried sex with a boyfriend. I got sick afterward. It took me several years before I finally experienced an orgasm. That boyfriend has been my only sexual partner, and he is now my husband.

The pain from the rape has been different than any other pain I have experienced. It left me curled up in a ball at night hurting too much to cry. It produced a gaping hole inside of me. And the pain fed the fear. I felt incomplete. It replaced other feelings. I felt different from everyone else. More than once I entertained the idea of suicide. At this point, eight years later, the pain is still a part of my life. I feel it whenever I am reminded of the rape. A scene in a movie can trigger it. The pain has given rise to anger that I direct at myself, the rapist, society, everything or nothing.

My feelings of self-doubt are very difficult to reprogram. I see my biggest problem as a lack of trust in myself and others. Before I was raped I was a very trusting person. Now, I have to work at it. The rape also sucked away what little confidence I had in myself. At times I convince myself that I am horrible, stupid, and incompetent. I blow negative comments way out of proportion and tend to ignore positive ones.

Through the muck of these problems, I have taken some positive steps. The first one in the transition from victim to survivor was to learn to defend myself. I have always been interested in the martial arts, and the rape accelerated my initiation into studying them. I now have a black belt in Tae Kwon Do. I know it is no guarantee, but it narrows the odds. I have used my knowledge to teach self-defense to others and to make them aware of the danger. Tae Kwon Do has taught me how to use my body and self-control. It has helped me to keep a handle on the fear. I also use it as a release for the pain and anger. It has given me confidence in myself.

I have also become an advocate for the local rape crisis center. I have given several presentations to church groups, junior high students, high school students, and students in alternative schools. I found this to be the most rewarding and healing thing I have done. I have told my story and the kids listen. It is tragic though because so many of them come up to me afterward and tell their stories. Or I can see it in their faces during the presentation—the shock and the pain.

My life has changed drastically because I was raped. I am trying to turn it around. I can't let him have the victory of destroying me. But more important, I am a good person and I deserve to let myself be happy.

Rebecca was on her way to Zimbabwe to serve in the Peace Corps when she first wrote her story. Upon her return, she decided to include an addendum:

My ten-year high school reunion is this year, a reminder that ten years have passed since I was raped. In these ten years, I have earned an associate of art degree, a bachelor's degree, and a master's degree. Along with my other accomplishments, each has brought me a step closer to healing myself. More than once, I have felt less than complete, but I am steadily approaching wholeness again. Each of us will take a different path for healing, but hope unites us all. Ten years may pass, but someday the cloud will lift and you can smile again. After all, you have already accomplished the hardest part—you survived.

6

The Rape on Independence Day

❮

The details of this woman's rape: "Eight years ago on the Fourth of July, as I lay sleeping in my house where I lived alone, a man broke in through an unlocked window. I awoke as he clamped his foul-smelling, gloved hand over my mouth. He then dragged me out of bed by my hair, held a knife to my neck, and threatened to kill me if I screamed. During the next several hours, he led me around my house, forced me to drink straight vodka, pulled my hair, alternated screaming with talking calmly, choked me until I nearly passed out, continued to threaten to kill me, and made it clear that I was not to try to look at him. In the process, my front teeth and something of my spirit were broken. He blindfolded me and led me to my bed, where I was beaten, sodomized, and raped vaginally. The following are some thoughts about how my life has changed since that Fourth of July."

When I hear about someone having been raped, I am no longer detached from it; it is my experience as well. And I no longer hear about a rapist without directly feeling a threat to my safety. Many people involved in the rape crisis movement believe that one in three women are sexually assaulted. So for every three women I know, one will be raped. And two won't be. I spent a lot of time thinking about which two women could have been spared from being raped because I had been raped. I would ask the universe to spare my sister, my mother, my friends—but how could I just protect *two* women when I wanted no other woman to experience the horror of rape? I gradually began to realize that I couldn't protect anyone else and that as long as I could be raped, anyone could.

At the age of thirty-seven, I am no longer naive about the possibility and consequences of the evil of a violent attack. I do not ever want to be violent toward another human being; I also do not want to be a victim. I now know much more about how to protect myself, but I have reached this point only after a painful struggle with my own potential for violence. Soon after being raped, I took a self-defense course that taught street-fighting techniques designed to maim and kill an attacker. I learned the techniques with a vengeance, so much so that I hurt an assistant instructor in one class by hitting him too hard. Although he wasn't seriously hurt, I cried about this incident for weeks because I had never believed in violence and didn't want to start resorting to it. Next I began the study of aikido, a Japanese form of self-defense, and grew to appreciate the philosophy of life and nonviolence it supports. I gradually realized, however, that it would not be an effective self-defense tool for me. I stopped thinking about self-defense and hoped I would never face violence directed at me again.

Then last year, a rash of rapes was occurring in my neighborhood. I took the basic Model Mugging course because I felt so frightened and angry. I also realized to my astonishment that I still had a place inside that was immobilized with terror, even though it had been seven years since the assault. I was still being raped in my head. Learning how to defend myself in the face of an attack helped free me in ways I hadn't anticipated. I am no longer being raped in my head. It's hard to put into words what that was like. I hadn't even realized it was happening. I had adjusted to a steady state of fear and feeling of powerlessness that went everywhere with me. I am no longer as afraid nor do I feel as powerless. I also have come to the conclusion that I can and will use the Model Mugging techniques to protect myself if I am attacked.

Despite confidence in my ability to defend myself, I am still easily frightened, and once frightened I require more time to recover. This was brought home to me recently. Around ten o'clock at night the lights went out suddenly and I became panicked. I ran out the front door, shaking and scared. My neighbors invited me in, and it became clear that the electricity was lost on the entire block. I sat in their house for about an hour and gradually calmed down enough to return to my house, armed with a pack of matches to help light my way. I had trouble falling asleep and still felt quite shaken and not myself the next day. It took at least twenty-four hours to recover.

I am no stranger to sleepless nights. Often I awaken at the time the assault began, and sometimes I awaken with a violent jump in my entire body. Because the rapist entered through a window, I cannot sleep with one open. I'd rather be hot than have a window open all night. A friend suggested that I install bars on my bedroom window, but I cannot imagine anything strong enough to help me feel safe.

Prior to being raped, I looked forward to vacationing alone and staying in hotels. For the last eight years, though, I simply did not go anywhere I would have to stay overnight alone in a hotel. I did not believe I could do it. Recently, however, when I missed the last flight out in an unfamiliar city, I learned that I can stay alone. But I would still do that as a last resort, not as a choice.

The image of the rapist sometimes invades my mind. Although I never saw him, I experience his brutal presence. It can pop up when I fantasize a romantic interlude or around the time of the year that the rape occurred. The Fourth of July has taken on a new meaning for me. It is not a time I look forward to—I often have memories, fears, and the experience of being raped again. Sometimes it is complete with the physical feelings associated with having been sodomized. This experience has gradually lessened over the years, but its intensity still surprises me when it does happen.

Sometimes I have unreasonable fears that my life will end abruptly, or I find I have no reason to be hopeful for the future. Sometimes I view death as a comfort.

I think of myself as a "raped woman" and have trouble ridding myself of this identity. Never having liked my body, I've carried a particular disdain for it since the assault. I especially hate my breasts and think of them as beaten and bruised, as they were during the assault. I was about twenty pounds overweight prior to being raped and I was never satisfied with my weight in any case. Since being raped, my weight has steadily increased. Although I have made numerous attempts to change my eating habits, I now weigh twenty pounds more than I did when I was raped and feel absolutely unable to lose the extra weight.

I am much less willing to spend time in relationships that are superficial. I don't get close to anyone without telling them about my experience of being raped. I've lost friends because they could not see me as anything but a victim. Telling my parents was especially hard. My mother initially could not understand me and my experience. She asked why I hadn't tried to "kick the rapist." I didn't tell her many details at first and she didn't know that he had a knife. She didn't know how scared I was or how alone. My sister helped her realize all of that. My sister was very helpful by listening when I wanted to talk. My brother and sister-in-law expressed concern and didn't seem to know what to do. My father just listened and didn't say much to me. I know now that he cursed the rapist and felt his own helplessness.

Never having been confident in romantic relationships, I am now not as willing to risk having one. The reason? I fear that I will be raped in a relationship, even a relationship of my choosing. My fear is not of a violent rape but of giving in to unwanted sexual advances. It would feel like rape to me even though a man wouldn't know that. Although I have attempted dating since being raped, I have had only one relationship, and it lasted two months. He was very responsive and kind, but I was never sure that I could depend on that lasting. I rather abruptly ended the relationship to the surprise and dismay of the man. I am at a loss to explain all the reasons I couldn't continue to see him, even though it's been five years.

Just as all of my relationships have changed, my relationship to God has changed as well. I used to believe that if I were "good" enough, God would protect me from "bad" things. I no longer believe that—I no longer look to God or anyone else to protect me or rescue me from the world. I believe that God gave all of us a free will to do as we so choose, which includes being violent or not. For this reason, I feel less naive and more able to deal with the occasional nastiness, or just the disappointments, that life sometimes throws at me. I do seek God often as a source of comfort and compassion in my life, and I see God in those with whom I am closest.

I think I am more real and more able to value the small, happy moments in life. I appreciate a kind word, a genuinely funny moment, a heartfelt honesty shared, and am more deeply touched by these things than before. I am not always able to sustain a positive outlook, but when I feel good, I am appreciative of life and all its gifts in a way I wasn't prior to being raped. A certain kind of innocence has been replaced by a more realistic, if sadder, view of the world.

7

From This Mountaintop

❨

Cynthia Carosella

I have written about the effects of rape three times—after three and one-half years, after seven, and now after nine. Each experience leaves me with more pages than the prior, but that is only because of the growth and new awarenesses that come with discovery. My association with the events of the rape almost feels like my association with the stories of the other contributors. I remember pain but not how it felt at the time. I remember being lost but not how it felt to be frustrated with my wanderings. I cry, but my tears are usually not tears of pain. They are tears of joy from sharing the possibilities that come with recovery and from realizing that dreams can come true and that our positions in this world are more complicated than they seem.

In hindsight, I realize that one of the best days of my life was November 29, 1991; I was laid off from my job on that day. While I could not imagine the merits of unemployment as I left my boss's office in tears, my only real problem was that I could not imagine. One by one, I called my family members, knowing I would get their empathy. When I called my sister, she asked, "If you could be doing anything in the world at this time, what would it be?" My reply was instantaneous. "Working on the book full-time." Her return was also without delay. "Okay. Because I know how much the book means to you, I'll support you until you finish it."

Initially, I declined. I grew up with the belief that if I accepted help from others, I was weak. A sense of independence had been instilled in me at an early age, and I had been supporting myself for over ten years. I had accepted money from my sister after I was raped, and I did not want her to have to help me again. But as the day wore on, I saw her generosity not as charity but as an incredible gift—the gift of freedom to focus solely on the book. In the three years since the conception of the idea, I had completed the equivalent of about three months of full-time work. My frustration with my slow pace coupled with my recent decision that I was "recovered" enough to seek contributors for the book convinced me that I should put aside my stubbornness and accept her offer. So many events had led me to that point.

It started nine years ago, on the day after I was raped, as I read in the Fourth of July edition of our newspaper about a twenty-one year old woman who had "allegedly" been raped at knifepoint while sleeping in her backyard. My overwhelming thought was of all the people I knew who would be reading the article and would not know that it was about me. I actually would have liked the story to have been on the front page and for my name to have been used. I wanted everyone to know what an awful thing had happened to me. In my despondency, it would have been so much easier to have people come to me with their support than for me to have to go to them for it. I felt this way because I did not experience any shame or blame from the rape.

But I could not grapple with the suddenness of falling from a state of well-being just hours before the rape to utter despair afterward. During the evening of the night I was raped, I had been jogging, high on endorphins, when the most beautiful full moon I had ever seen made its appearance on the horizon. This moon seemed at least twenty times its usual size and it was gold. I was convinced that it had skipped its orbit and had taken up another much closer. I'll admit that at times I am overly romantic. With a name that means moon goddess, I could not resist the idea of sleeping outside that night.

Even though the rape was not the first traumatic event I had faced in my life, it brought me to a point so low that I knew I could not simply try to recover as I would from the flu. My first anxiety attack and my inability to eat anything other than toast for two weeks were warning signs that I needed outside help. Rape felt like a sword had pierced through every layer of my skin, flesh, and bone and on to my core, leaving a virulent solution that seeped into my soul. If I decided to forget that the rape had ever happened, I would have effectively been giving myself a couple of epidermal stitches, leaving the rest of the wound to boil below the surface. I knew I needed treatment that could reach my core.

I took advantage of what was available for rape victims in my community—I joined the support group through the rape crisis center and I went into private therapy that was funded by the victim witness assistance program. I thought that this was a good start. I then resumed my life as a student and changed my course load to include women's studies classes. In addition, I tried hypnotherapy to reduce the size of the cloud in my head and isolation tank therapy to tune into the inner workings of my mind. I had already taken self-defense classes before I was raped. While I did not attempt to use these techniques because of the knife, I did successfully defend myself against an attacker just one month before the rape.

Initially I tried to work recovery into my life as I would a dentist appointment. I discounted the energy and focus required to recover. I did not realize that recovery from rape is a full-time job; I only realized that I had little interest in my education when I hurt so badly.

I saw the world around me continue at its fast pace, seeming to ignore me. The harder I tried to keep up, the further I fell behind. Nobody had warned me that life after rape was going to be like this. Even my therapist was of little assistance. Her belief that I was having a difficult time because of my Catholic upbringing convinced me that psychoanalysis was not what I needed at that time. Then the rapist tried to intimidate me—he showed up in the same lane at the university swimming pool and at the next table in the library. He had not been charged because of a technicality, so the police told me there was nothing they could do unless he threatened me. Alcohol and thoughts of suicide were easy escapes, but I always stopped at just the thoughts—I could not allow the rapist's opinion of me to determine my opinion of myself.

My need for escape brought me on what I have come to refer to as my "migrations"—flights from the familiar to the unfamiliar for the purposes of exploration and discovery. I believed that the world known to me did not contain what I was seeking. I wanted to feel balanced and positive as I had before the rape. It became necessary to venture to other realms of the world and to other realms of my "self."

I have always used synchronicity as an indicator that I am "on the right track" and that much more is happening in my life than I am aware of. The universe makes sense to me in these moments, which remind me that I am not simply plodding along aimlessly.

Through a series of synchronistic events, I found myself on a plane headed to the South Pacific with two friends. But because of unforeseen complications, which included one friend contracting typhoid fever in Indonesia, I ended up traveling alone for two months in New Zealand. A lovelier place and a lovelier people I cannot imagine. For the first time since I had been raped, I knew that I was where I was supposed to be—the moments of synchronicity were almost too numerous to count.

I also experienced four life-threatening situations within the first month of being there: Because of a sudden gust of wind, my plane nearly crashed when I first arrived. I was caught in a landslide while doing some field research and came within twenty feet of being smashed by a large boulder. The next day I was chased across a field by a raging bull. (I still laugh when I picture myself running, holding my journal over my rear end as a shield against spiked horns.) I escaped over a fence before he caught up with me. Then I got lost in a snowstorm while hiking with inadequate gear but managed to reach my destination. These events all hold something in common—they taught me that I was a survivor! I had not thought of myself in that respect after the rape—I had focused on the misfortune of being raped and not on the fortune of being alive. In New Zealand, nature's tests provided this answer without any negative repercussions and reminded me that my strength does not always come in a physical form.

The last incident, in particular, forced me to tap into a source of strength that I had forgotten about. I had left the town at the base of Mount Cook, New Zealand's highest peak, late in the day, heading for an overnight stay at a cabin along the trail. Even though I rushed, I had not found the cabin by nightfall. Then it began to snow. I could not see the trail markers to follow the trail in either direction, and I did not have the gear to protect myself from the elements all night. Somehow I found the strength to persevere and not give up. Even though I was often fooled by large boulders that from a distance appeared to be the cabin, I was determined to search until I found it. I experienced various levels of fear, but I persisted. I tried to remain calm and to believe in myself. I knew that I could not give up. *I wanted to live, just as I wanted to live that night I was raped.* Just as I did what I had to do that night to remain alive, I used all of my senses as a guide. Seeing that cabin is one sight I will never forget. Even though the radio and inside light did not work, I reveled in the safety that its four walls provided me and slept with the peace that survival had brought me.

Two days later, I left the cabin and headed back down the trail. At one point, I entered a clearing of rocks and saw before me a free-standing stone arch. It had not been there on the way up. As I approached it, I realized that it was not physically there; I was the only one who was seeing it. A voice inside of me told me that passing through it would represent my entrance into a new realm of my life. As I did so, the alpine parrots flew over-head—they were real. This vision sustains my belief in a universe that has a purpose.

As life would have it, I arrived back home on July third, exactly two years after I was raped. All other flights a week before and after this date were full. I returned with new aware-nesses and the feeling that something really big was going to hap-pen. Unfortunately I learned that no matter how much I wanted to create a better life, I was returning to one of unresolved issues. My outlook had changed, but familiar surroundings meant famil-iar routines. I was faced with the distractions of working full-time to pay off credit card bills from the trip and of going to school full-time. There was no time to think about my dreams, much less recovery. For a year and a half, I always "just got by"—just enough money to pay the bills and just enough studying to get passing grades.

About a month before I graduated, a friend called with some bad news. She had just been told by her physician that she had a facial fracture that had gone undetected six years before when she was beaten and raped. She would have to have an operation to repair it. This would mean medical expenses beyond what her insurance would pay, time off from work, arrangements with friends to care for her after she left the hospital, not to mention the pain.

I was very upset to think that the attack could still be affecting her in this way six years later. This was an impetus for me to look at myself and consider if rape was still affecting my life. I sat down with the intent of writing down every way that I recognized the rape still impacted my life. Two hours and thirty-seven ways later, I had a list that eventually expanded to fifty-seven ways over the following weeks. "Fear of the dark" was first on the list, followed by "fear of sleeping outside," "loss of desire to make myself look nice," "loss of desire to help others." Most notable was the apparent loss of what I referred to as my "social self." It was the "me" that trusted, that did not judge others, that could easily produce a smile for just about anyone, that loved to have a good time as long as everyone else was, that felt so full of life I could give it away to others.

The operation was not a success. It was to have been an outpatient procedure, but my friend ended up in intensive care for three days. While there, she heard one of the nurses refer to her as a "baby" for requiring special care for a seemingly simple surgery.

At that time, I headed for a bookstore to find some answers for both of us, something that could double as a get-well present for her. Searching for answers that are not to be found is frustrating until one realizes that perhaps she is part of the solution. After finding nothing that addressed the long-term effects of rape, I glanced once more at the shelves and briefly saw my name on the spine of a book. I laughed. Another vision that was trying to tell me something?

My list of long-term effects grew to fifty-eight—"need to put together book about the long-term effects of rape." While I was trying to reduce the size of the list instead of increasing it, this effect would reduce the impact of the other fifty-seven.

As I spoke with those I knew who had been raped, my conviction that this book was needed grew. Just the initial stages of researching the topic and what is involved in putting a book together had a positive effect on my self-image. An indicator for me was that my teeth being crooked began to annoy me. I had not been concerned with them since before I was raped, but suddenly I had to do something to correct the problem. I embarked on a long-term treatment plan and followed it as money allowed.

The steps that I should take to create the book were very apparent to me from the beginning. And I kept meeting people who offered the right advice when I needed it. But once again the day-to-day distraction of working to pay the bills left little energy for anything else. I did not realize it at the time, but my snail's pace resulted from my attempting to hold down three full-time jobs. In addition to my paying job, the work on the book had reintroduced me to the full-time job of recovery. So while I may not have been making steady progress on the book, my list of long-term effects was shrinking.

After accepting my sister's offer, I had the opportunity to go on more migrations, seeking answers from others who also recognized the lack of information concerning the long-term effects of rape and were willing to contribute what they knew.

Initially I believed that I would have to give a lot of myself in the process of collecting stories. What I did not expect was to receive so much support, encouragement, sense of purpose, and love from the contributors. I did face many tears, but I learned that tears often bring smiles that reflect the release of secrets hidden for years. And I learned I am happiest doing work that is beneficial to all involved—I was aiding others as they brought me the answers I sought.

Despite these benefits, I still felt great sadness over the apparent loss of the social "me." I did not know if it was still inside of me or if it was forced out and replaced by a part that had to be armored at all times.

Here the power of synchronicity again proved itself. It led me to a workshop in which breath work and bioenergetics were used to "shake up and release" that which builds up inside of us. The group leader told me that she was going to help me release the rage inside of me. "What rage?" I asked. "The rage from the rape," she replied. "I'm not sure I have any left in me." "Let's check it out and see."

I had never really expressed my anger from the rape. I had buried it deep inside. I might have connected with it when I saw injustices being done to someone else, but I can't remember a time in which I really let it out.

The exercises the group leader took me through led me on an internal migration, to realms of my "self" I had yet to explore.

I found myself reliving the rape, but this time *I got to fight back*. I unleashed eight years of pent-up anger. I screamed and made sounds that never before had come out of me. I was pushing and kicking and resisting. Four people worked against me by trying to hold me down. They were no match! When it was over, the virulent fluid had seeped out and was reduced to sweat that soaked my clothing.

Following this release, I found myself in a peaceful trance. It was the first time in my life that I experienced total calm. In my mind, I was witnessing a reenactment of the night I was raped from the point at which I first discovered the full moon. A figure entered my field of vision from the right. It was me—I was observing myself walk by, only I was gold just like the moon and I was happy and smiling just as I had been before I was raped. I pranced by and just as I was wondering where the gold "me" was going, she turned and looked at me. In her golden face, I saw the "me" that I had been missing since the day I was raped, the "embodiment" of my missing part. Then the gold "me" smiled at me and reached her golden fingers toward me. I instinctively reached out to her, and in a touch as dramatic as that in Michelangelo's *The Creation of Adam*, I knew I once again was whole. The golden me had been a prisoner of my rage. Releasing the rage released her. It was as if anger had smothered the part of me I missed, just as the rapist had smothered me with my pillow.

Whereas I used to believe that the release of my rage was not something that I needed, I now know that it had to happen in order for me to progress. Rage did not disappear after eight years; in fact, it was still quite raw. I had associated rage with violence and unattractiveness. Wonder of wonders, my release of it has made me whole again. I toy with the idea that my next project will be to open a Rage-o-rama where anyone can go to release the buildup of rage that is a part of most of us.

When I look in the mirror now, I see a culmination of all that has happened to me. My new smile manifests the physical expression of my happiness at having reached a balance in my life again. I rarely think of myself as someone who has been raped. Rape no longer serves as a qualifier of who I am. I never want to be introduced as a rape victim. And the only aspect of the rape that brings me back to it is the memory of the sound of my mother's voice through the telephone line when my sister told her I had been raped, the sound of a mother experiencing one of her worst fears. I know contentment as I work in my office, perched among the pines on a mountaintop. I am here because I have learned that I can make my dreams come true.

Shortly after deciding that I wanted to live in the mountains, I met a man who had recently decided to build his dream house in the mountains. I asked him if there was anything in his design that was especially exciting to him. "Oh yes. There is a sleeping porch on the second story. I love to sleep outside under the moon and stars. The sleeping porch will allow me to do it safely." I had more than a hunch that I would be there with him. So now we sleep outside on a mountaintop, slightly closer to the moon, but far above the fear I left below. Sometimes the best gifts do not even have to be given.

I have learned to trust my intuition. I learned to do what it was telling me even if it did not make sense, even if it meant doing something that I did not want to do, such as asking for help. I have learned that accepting help means I am strong enough to know that I needed it. I can go so much farther when others are around to lighten the load. And I consider myself fortunate to have family and friends who offer help, many times without being asked.

Beyond the gift of money, my sister empowered me with her unfailing belief that I would accomplish what I set out to do. Her gift was the water that nurtured a seedling into a flowering plant. These chapters are the fruits. I invite you to pick them. After the fruit has nourished you, find the source of water, the spring of life, that will transform your seed into another flowering plant.

8

Why Couldn't
I Cry?

❝

Lisa was raped nine years ago at the age of eighteen. Dealing with the effects of rape was not something she thought would be required just two weeks into her freshman year of college.

I thought college was going to be the most positive and powerful experience of my lifetime. Little did I know that, instead, it would mark the beginning of a nightmare. I was excited about going to parties and meeting new people. When I met James I felt that he was someone I could trust. The women on my dormitory floor liked him, and they seemed glad we had met. When James asked me to a party the following weekend, I was thrilled. I believed that I was starting to fit in and adjust to college life.

I went to the party and James was there. He asked me to dance and I said yes. While we were dancing I could see the women from my floor cheering us on. We drank while we were dancing and I was having a great time. At one point James asked me if I wanted to go back to his room; the music was too loud for conversation. I said yes because we had been yelling in order to hear each other. We went to his room and continued to drink. He asked his roommate to leave the room and he did.

James then sat down next to me on the couch and poured me another beer. Then he began kissing me. I enjoyed kissing him and I felt comfortable with him. However, that comfort soon turned to fright when he wanted to go further and I said no. I didn't know how to stop him. He was so much bigger than me. I tried to get him off of me. I told him to stop, but he did not listen; instead, he forced me to have sex against my will. He raped me *and* took away my virginity in one violent act.

When it was over, he told me that he had a good time and that he wanted to see me again. I could not believe he was actually saying those things to me. I just wanted everything to go away. I wanted to forget it all. With my body hurting, somehow I made it back to my room. The pain was horrible, but I could not cry. I took a shower and tried to go to sleep and pretend the rape never happened.

The next morning, the women on my floor came into my room, exclaiming how great it was that James and I left the party together. They all told me what a great guy James was and how lucky I was to have scored with him. Even more difficult was hearing similar praise from the resident advisor. I was hurt and confused. They all assumed I had consensual sex and that I was fine. Not one of them asked me what happened, not even my RA. She was supposed to be the one person I could trust and talk to.

I told myself that I would not reveal to anyone what really happened. I would deal with it myself. After all, I was drinking that night and I went up to his room, so I thought that I must have led him on.

A self-destructive pattern followed. I abused alcohol to escape and relax. I ate enormous amounts of food because I believed that the rape would not have occurred if I had been heavier. I managed to put on fifty to sixty pounds in a year's time. I wasn't sure who I was or what I was doing. Eventually I rationalized that because I had already dealt with many issues in my life, I could figure out this one too. I convinced myself that because I could not cry, the rape must not have been that bad. At least that is what I remember telling myself.

Then the nightmares began. I also found that whenever I tried to be intimate with another person, I had flashbacks of the rape. James was everywhere. If I saw a man on campus who looked like him, I would get scared. James did actually try to contact me again, but I avoided him. I had a class with him my sophomore year, but I don't remember going to that class much.

My senior year I began dating Tim. I loved him and liked that he seemed dependent on me. Through him I managed to avoid dealing with my own problems. We maintained a long-distance relationship while I attended graduate school out of state, and after I graduated we were married.

Once we began living together the nightmares were an almost nightly occurrence. Tim never forced me to have sex, but the pressure to have it was intense. Sex was something I desperately wanted to avoid, and it was painful to know that while I loved him, I could not enjoy physical intimacy with him. Every time he touched me, I was afraid he would want more than I did. Tim knew that our attempts at lovemaking were difficult for me, and he became frustrated. I finally figured out why our long-distance relationship had worked so well—it had freed me from having to deal with the issue at all.

I finally reached a point where I decided that I could no longer keep the secret to myself. People who looked like James were still triggering flashbacks, and I was pushing my husband away. I was drinking more and I knew things were getting out of control fast.

After six years, I broke my silence by telling my best friend, Becky. She just held me and cried. I remember feeling lonely and helpless because I still could not cry despite the intense pain. I knew it was time to see a professional; life had to get better before I hurt myself or anyone else. So I went and talked with Joan, a therapist. She listened to my story and assured me that I was not responsible for what James did to me. Hearing those words was such a relief: I was not responsible! All of the messages that society gave me had led me to believe I was responsible.

With Joan's help I was able to tell Tim about the rape. It was difficult for him to accept that our marriage was different because of James. He stood by me though and was a tremendous supporter. Some nights I woke up screaming and others I kicked him out of bed, but he was determined to stay and work things through.

Eventually, through my own recovery process I was able to

take back some of the power and control James had over me. He was no longer in my dreams and he was not always in my thoughts. The face that had been controlling my life began to fade. I was able to stop abusing alcohol and to lose the weight that I had gained. Now I exercise and eat healthy foods. My therapist helped me to realize that I do have the skills to cope with my feelings; I no longer needed to rely on alcohol for that.

I am now able to take responsibility for the choices I made the night of the rape. I accept responsibility for drinking that night, for going to his room that night, and for wanting us to kiss. But, I will *never* take responsibility for the rape. That was his choice, not mine.

I also realized through my recovery process that I needed to start being honest with myself. This meant dealing with my marriage to Tim and my true feelings for him. I no longer wanted him to be dependent on me, and I began to crave a feeling of independence for myself. Once I reached that conclusion, I knew that my marriage needed to end.

Telling Tim that I no longer felt we could be husband and wife was one of the most difficult things I have done. He left that night and we were divorced six months later. He is no longer my husband, but he is still my best friend. I know he will always blame James for our marriage not working.

As for me, I know I can never change what happened that night, but I can move on with my life. Part of that process is becoming much more aware and active. I now get angry when I hear about the court system "revictimizing" victims. I get angry at television and movie producers who portray rape as anything but an act of violence. I get angry when I see sexist commercials and advertisements. And I almost threw up while watching the Clarence Thomas hearings. All of these things are a part of who I am now. I do not hate men, but I do believe that men need to take responsibility for helping stop violence against women.

It was important to me to find a release for all of these feelings, especially the anger. I have become an educator, telling my story to high school and college students so that women will know they are not alone and men will think twice before forcing a woman to have sex. I also work as a sexual assault victim's advocate because I know it is a terrifying thing to go through alone. If there had been an advocate program at my college, I believe things would have been very different for me.

I am a nonviolent person, but sometimes I get concerned about the anger I still feel toward James. Because of him, my future intimate relationships will always be different. It takes me a long time to trust and to feel truly safe in a relationship, and I know the only way I can be happy in a relationship is to feel safe. If only we lived in a safe world. Since we don't, I do my part to make it the safest place it can be for women and children.

9

My Victory Lap: The Gift of Life

❡

Carol R. Simonson

Carol, a forty-year-old business woman, discusses the importance of the support of her colleagues, friends, family, and therapist to her recovery. Some of the best advice she received came from her therapist: "You can live or die. The choice is yours."

She writes, "One of the ways my spirit hung on and ultimately flourished was through writing. I kept a journal and wrote whenever needed, zealously at times. It was my lifeline; it was a method of private processing. And it has provided a record that gives me perspective and the strength to go on. So it only seemed fitting to write my story for this book in my journal. Longhand. Slowly. Just as it has unfolded over the past nine years."

When I decided to stay home from a planned backpacking trip that August weekend in 1984 to watch the first Olympic women's marathon, it was inconceivable to me that I would do so with a crushed body and soul under the supervision of a psychotherapist. "It can never happen to me" happened in a brutally violent way the night before.

Sleepless and numb with pain, my only goal for the day was to watch the marathon. My mind could not follow the analytical commentary. Yet I will never forget the look on Joan Benoit's face as she led the race from start to finish. Especially vivid is my image of her running all alone on a Los Angeles freeway, surrounded only by miles of concrete. She was a picture of total focus and determination. This image, forever etched in my subconscious, became my first step on the road back.

I was thirty-one years old at the time, an aspiring financial analyst and just about to celebrate the first anniversary of buying my first home. I was on a roll.

———

What unfolded was very unreal; surely it could only happen in the movies. I had turned the TV off after watching the gymnastics competition and gone to bed. In the middle of the night, I awoke with a pillow over my head, unable to breathe. After a brief struggle, I knew I was hopelessly at the mercy of the intruder. When the terror of what followed became unbearable and I began to think I'd rather die, I remember thinking to myself, No! I will do whatever it takes to survive. In that moment, I detached my mind from my body. And I survived.

———

I had survived, but never had I felt so lifeless. In a matter of minutes, I went from a competent, high-functioning woman, capable of completing complex financial analyses, to one who stuttered and rocked back and forth, unable to complete thoughts or sentences. I could not focus or concentrate. I was a prisoner of flashback after flashback. Most days I had to drag myself out of bed. I could not drive a car. I could not run. I was afraid to go outside. The soreness of my physical wounds penetrated to every bone in my body. As my body was broken, so too was my spirit.

What follows is the rest of my story, which very painfully and very slowly became one of hope, in spite of setbacks. A year and a half after the rape, my perpetrator was caught and much of the pain and horror resurfaced as I went through the police lineup and legal process. In spite of such setbacks along the way, the reclamation of my life continued and my spirit somehow persevered.

Now, years later, as a chief financial officer, with running medals hanging in the den of a much larger home, it is my recovery that I am most proud of. My job title, my house, and my other accomplishments are only important to the degree that they provide some tangible evidence to other survivors that you too can come back. You can reclaim your life.

In writing my story and really wanting my contribution to be useful and to make a difference, I asked myself, What made the difference for me? I could point to three things. First, I did not have to worry about losing my job. Second, I had the unconditional support of friends and family. Third, I had a role model I could trust who was a rape survivor.

As a single woman with my first house and monthly mortgage payments, my well-paying job was essential. How fortunate I was to work for a supportive company and remarkable boss, Bobbi. After consulting with the executive officers at our company, she told me that they and the company would do whatever it took to get me whole and functioning again. I was given my full paycheck, without deductions for sick time or vacation time, for as long as I was off work. She told me they would help pay for therapy. She told me not to worry.

Though tears were streaming down my face and my body was shaking with fear, I felt as if a thousand pounds, no, the weight of the world, had been lifted from my shoulders. If Bobbi had told me to take some time off but to pull myself together, or if she had given me just enough time for my physical wounds to heal, I would have failed miserably. With her full support though, my panic was calmed. I could focus all of my attention and energy on getting well.

No one wanted to bounce back more than I, but my biggest fear was that my mind would not work the same. Immediately after the rape, I could not rely on it to process information. I share this because it is important for those affected by rape to understand there is a mind/body connection. Somehow the wiring comes undone following trauma. "Pulling myself together" and functioning as I had before simply were not possible.

What Bobbi did next was nothing short of brilliant. She talked to a psychotherapist about how to deal with me. She wanted to know what she should do to encourage me to come back and once back what she could do to help me to function successfully in my job. With guidance, she met with my immediate work group, told them what had happened and counseled them on how to treat me when I came back.

I'll never forget my first day back. I came in early so no one would see me. I was afraid to look anyone in the eye: I didn't know what to say to them, and I was afraid of what they might say. I went up the back stairs instead of taking the elevator and managed to get into my office without running into anyone. I remember the relief was short-lived when I found I just couldn't understand the projects on my desk—things I knew I had completed before the rape. I was immobilized with fear and lost in a fog as I desperately tried to connect to my work and my surroundings.

And so it was. It was slow, painfully slow, and sometimes just painful. There were many days when I burst into tears for no apparent reason and had to go home. I felt exhausted most of the time.

Through it all, Bobbi's support and the support of my work group made all the difference. They treated me just as before and told me how great it was to have me back. They never once asked about the rape. I never felt pitied; I never felt as if I was being treated with kid gloves. What I felt from them was simple care and authenticity. They also gave me space to get well. The rest of the company followed their example.

Seven months later I received a promotion to finance manager in another part of the company. This victory was all the more sweet in that my new boss did not know what had happened to me—I would have a clean slate. My confidence soared in new surroundings, immersed in new projects that contained no reminders.

As essential to my healing was the support and compassion of friends and family. Two women friends took me into their home when I knew I could never go back to mine. I felt safe and welcomed. They didn't push. They didn't prod. They didn't give me pep talks. They just let me be. If I needed to cry, they let me cry without trying to "make it all better."

Another incremental shift in my healing occurred when I reluctantly decided to go ahead and take a planned trip to the Grand Canyon. Still fragile, both physically and mentally, I wasn't sure if I was ready for the rigorous three-day hike this trip would entail. It was with the support of another friend that I finally agreed to take the risk.

There were many gifts that came from that trip. The biggest was reclaiming my physical power and my mental tenacity in accomplishing a very specific goal. It boosted my confidence in a way that transferred to other aspects of my life once I arrived back home. Getting away from everything and being around people who had no idea what had happened to me also helped enormously. When I realized there was no *R* emblazoned on my forehead and people were treating me normally, I was filled with joy and hope. It was the first time I let out a full-belly laugh since the rape. Playing had never felt so good. I experienced the first period of time without flashbacks.

Then there was Mom. She flew out from California to take care of me. She was the one who helped me navigate my way through the difficult first days of therapy and the humiliating tests at the public health department. She helped me make lists that brought me back to the real world. Call the realtor. Call my boss. She drove the car alongside of me so I would feel safe the first time I ran again.

Finally, having a role model who was also a survivor of rape was a huge help to me. When I sat across from my therapist, Mary Ellen, I saw a highly competent, high-functioning woman. She shared her story, so I knew she had been in the same black despair that I was. And yet there she was—so together. She had come back. I could too.

I trusted her when she told me my mind would work again as it had before. I must have asked her a hundred times, "Are you sure? Do you promise?" I trusted her when she said it was OK to look in every closet and under every bed if it helped me to feel safe. I trusted her when she said it was OK to look behind me when I ran, as many times as I wanted. I trusted her when she told me not to fight the flashbacks. I trusted her advice not to read the newspapers or go to violent movies.

I know I would have reacted differently had this advice come from anyone other than a survivor of rape. I would have questioned it, worried I was being weak or even downright silly. With Mary Ellen all of the energy that would have gone into second-guessing myself was channeled instead into getting better.

So I write this for survivors, bosses, mothers and fathers, family and friends and for those who can move beyond the experiences of rape to become role models. In this way, the healing process comes full circle and continues in the most powerful way.

> The secret of change is to focus all your energy not on fighting the old, but on building the new.
>
> Way of the Peaceful Warrior
> Dan Millman

I have changed. I am different now.

I stop and smell the roses more. Not a day goes by that I don't appreciate being alive. I see life as a fragile, miraculous gift.

I respond much more gracefully when little things go wrong. And when seemingly big things go wrong, I cope differently than before. Instead of panic, or even fear, my reaction is, "Oh, well. What do I need to do to get myself out of this mess?"

I know that spiritual growth is real and I trust the universe more.

Ironically, I don't need to be in control as much in my personal and professional life. While I will never be a "type B," I am certainly a much more mellowed "type A."

One of my goals was to run in the Boston Marathon. The rape made me more determined to accomplish this goal. On a certain level, it was a way to reclaim my life and spirit. I was successful on my third attempt to qualify and ran the Boston Marathon on April 17, 1989. It was a victory lap I'll never forget!

I live my life knowing I will always have flashbacks. Happily, with time they are less painful, almost like watching TV.

I work with rape survivors as a volunteer for Outward Bound. It is very important to me to give back. I discovered pleasure and priority in empowering others.

My life will never be the same, but after nine years, I feel I have transformed the rape into more "positives" than "negatives." It is a cruel gift, but nonetheless, a gift.

I am better able to "fall apart" and ask for support from family and friends. I ask to be walked to my car. I ask to have a friend wait until I'm inside my front door. It is refreshing to understand in a new way that being strong doesn't mean you can't ask for help or hugs. I never hesitate to ask.

I experienced a full-body rush of joy that could hardly be contained when, six years after the rape, a friend who didn't know of my past told me I was the most mentally healthy person he knew. I measure my accomplishments differently. Formerly, success meant "getting A's" and "achieving." Now I measure success by the quality of the journey.

And so the journey continues. As I've come to learn of life as a process, so too is healing and wellness. I must continue to make friends with fear and to expand my awareness in order to stay on the path of growth. I am so very grateful for the gift of life!

10

Tarred & Feathered

☽

"THE DEMONS ARE LOOSE; THAT IS THE ONLY WAY THEY CAN FLY AWAY."

S., a twenty-four-year-old actor, writer, and model, refers to herself as Pandora's Roommate. In addition to childhood abuse, drug usage, and promiscuity, she has dealt with the effects of being raped by a stranger at the age of fifteen and a partner at the age of eighteen. As a means of healing, she surrounds herself with friends, writing, dancing, and acting, and she has vowed never to forget how far she has come in her recovery process. "If I do, I know I will be opening myself up for the same thing." She is currently completing a play about her experiences.

TARRED & FEATHERED

A little girl cries in the darkness so nobody can see
The door flies open; a voice whispers, "come & sit on Daddy's
  knee"
Right away, the barrier grows, and in her head she hides
Daddy says he loves her with humiliation—he's bleeding her
  inside
No love is made from secrets. No love is made with tears
Mother brings no consolation—she's lived with it for years
Her friends respond with laughter. Her teachers, they deny:
"You don't have a case, except imagination, without proof."
What about her cries?

She doesn't know about love or understanding. But she's learned
  to connive,
The system has tarred and feathered this little girl at the age of
  five.

The silhouette of a beautiful woman rushes past the avenue
Her work is done. The sun is down. But her day is far from
  through
It's a night for solo wilding as a man follows her around
She forgets to look for a moment, and he throws her to the
  ground
Shaking in the 27th precinct, her tale of fear unfolds
Unwanted possession and violation. The policeman's eyes grow
  cold:
"Are you sure you weren't asking for trouble? didn't try to turn
  him on?"
No more to lose, except self-respect; the law says there's nothing
  to go on

Stripped of all her soul and pride on the news today
The system has tarred and feathered this woman, not the man
    who got away

What about our freedom? What about our rights?
Will we ever save the innocent? Will we ever feel safe at night?

11

On the Inside Looking Out

❆

This woman describes herself as someone who enjoyed life, her friends, spontaneous laughter, and her first semester of college— before she was raped by a date twelve years ago. Now twenty-nine, she discusses the losses she has experienced since the rape: loss of control, loss of trust, loss of self-esteem, and loss of opportunity to have healthy sexual relations.

For several years after being raped, I was terrified to share my experience with anyone. It was only after I began writing this story two years ago that I was able to tell some of my close friends. The first person I told was a friend who I knew would not judge or criticize. It was frightening at first, but then wonderful to have her express such support, empathy, and care. I was then able to share my story with other friends. There are others who I choose not to tell, as they have been narrow-minded, judgmental, and unsupportive in other instances, and I did not want to take the risk of being misunderstood. It is very strengthening to me, however, knowing that it is a matter of choice for me now, rather than a secret that I must keep inside. Now each time I share my story with someone, I feel myself more and more healed and empowered.

For about seven years after the rape, I felt I was on the inside looking out. It was as if I was watching others really live their lives but I was not allowing myself to do that. I became an observer. I feared and denied feelings that were pent up inside me, feelings that desperately wanted to be let out, to be expressed and dealt with. Later I would find that once I began identifying and expressing my feelings, I could become a participant in life again.

Even as a child I learned to keep my feelings to myself, since expressing them was not done in my family. After the rape, I continued to bury all of my emotions. I denied that it even happened for quite some time and did not want to face the hurt, anger, sadness, and fear. It was eating away at me though. I felt anger at a man who sexually violated my rights through a violent criminal act, even though I continually said no. My sadness and hurt were those of an innocent girl who kept this terrible thing a secret, fearing peers' judgments and my own emotions. I was sad for all the things that were taken from me—my innocence, my ability to trust myself and others, my self-esteem, and my ability to have healthy relationships with others. I desperately feared for my life. I remember wondering if this man would spare my life or if my dead body would be found in some isolated area.

When any of these feelings did come to the surface, I refused to deal with them. Even my feelings of genuine happiness were withheld. I was unable to laugh spontaneously or enjoy my life. I only laughed when I felt I *should,* and then it was often artificial.

Only in the last few years have I acknowledged the tremendous effect the rape has had on my life. Some of the effects are:

Feeling responsible and guilty For some time it was difficult for me to acknowledge that I was raped. Like many rape victims, I carried around a great deal of guilt and shame for my part in what happened to me. Even though in my rational mind I knew that I was not at fault, I couldn't help feeling responsible for going out on that date. For a long time, I felt that I had deserved to be treated that way.

Feeling a loss of control The rape made me feel as though someone had taken all of my control—over my body, my choices, and what others could do to me. Prior to the rape I had always felt a great sense of control; I had tried since the age of eleven to take care of myself and my own feelings, and told myself that I didn't need the help of others, especially my family. The rape reinforced my strong need for control. For example, a friend who was spending the weekend with me offered to cook lunch for us, allowing me to relax. However, I became panic-stricken when I didn't have control over the kitchen (my domain), and I couldn't stop telling my friend how to do things the right way (my way).

Spontaneity to me is a way of losing control, therefore it takes a great deal of conscious effort for me to let go. I plan everything out, including all of the intricate details. I find it amusing, yet frustrating that I actually catch myself planning to be spontaneous. I continue to work at this and realize that in certain situations it is all right to lose control. However, I still fear having it taken from me against my will.

Feeling a loss of trust I lost faith that others would trust or believe me. I questioned my own judgment and trusted neither myself nor others. I feared that if I told people, they would only place more guilt, shame, and responsibility on me in addition to what I had already placed on myself.

I also distanced myself even more from my family. I felt my mother, in particular, would place a great deal of blame on me and criticize my judgment, as she had done throughout my childhood. I was afraid she might punish me by making me quit college or move back home. I can easily imagine her saying, "See, you're just not responsible enough to be out on your own." I have never told any member of my family about the rape, and I am not sure that I ever will.

My ability to trust men, in particular, was severely affected. I thought they were continually lying to me, and I could not accept a compliment without questioning the motive behind it. Even my behavior toward men who were just casual acquaintances was affected. I found myself being rude and guarded when I didn't know a man well, and I always assumed that men had ulterior motives for trying to get to know me better. I feared that they were trying to gain my trust so that they too could rape me. Sometimes I would actually plot ways to turn men off or to make them dislike me so I could protect myself from any abuse. This also helped reinforce the idea that men could not possibly like me for who I was.

Feeling a loss of self-esteem After the rape, my self-worth plummeted. I didn't think I deserved to have a loving, sensitive man who cared for me. Instead, I thought I deserved to be treated with no respect, as if I were wearing a scarlet letter. A truly healthy relationship with a man was not in the scope of my imagination.

I'd had very few relationships with men (and no sexual relationships) prior to the rape. After, I sometimes dated men, even though I may not have felt any true attraction or interest in them. I did not believe I had choices and thought that if a man expressed interest in me, I had better go out with him regardless. It was as if I said to myself, I have to take what I can get. Why would someone honorable and decent want someone like me?

Often I dated men for whom I felt pity, and in some way I tried to step into a role in which I felt needed. This role was like a bargain with the world: I would date men with problems because (1) that is who I deserved; (2) I might possibly be able to help them; which in turn would (3) make me feel accepted by them. I yearned to be accepted by a man for who I was. Now I know that would have been impossible to accomplish at that time, because I was not accepting of myself. When I did date a man who may have genuinely cared about me, I would automatically back off and withdraw as soon as he began getting close. I did this, hoping that he would dislike my response and end the relationship. My reasoning was: Forcing the man to break up with me once again reinforced my belief that no man was truly interested in me for who I was. Ultimately, I feared that if I really allowed a man to get to know me, he would come to dislike what he saw. This gave me more ammunition in convincing myself that I was a failure and unworthy of a decent man.

Feeling a loss of opportunity to have healthy sexual relationships My ability to deal with sexual relationships in a healthy manner was extremely damaged by the rape. At first I was absolutely petrified of sex and would find any means of avoiding it. I found it very convenient to pass out or fall asleep when things got out of the comfort range. A few years after the rape, however, I started feeling as if the only way in which a man would accept me was through sex.

Seven years after the rape these feelings and effects continued to eat away at me. I became more and more depressed and withdrawn. At first I blamed it on my job, which I hated, but knew that it was more than that; I was not happy inside. While I still wasn't prepared to change the way I dealt with my emotions, I thought I might be able to find a quick fix for my depression.

I finally sought help from the counseling referral service offered at my company. I couldn't believe how quickly the counselor was able to learn so much about me. After our first session, she referred me to a therapist in private practice. Being so out of touch with my feelings at the time, I wasn't sure why she thought I needed therapy (even though I had told her about the rape). It was still hard for me to accept that I needed help. Shortly after starting work with the therapist, however, I realized my feelings about the rape needed to be identified and expressed and I knew I couldn't do it by myself.

The relationship I am in now is very healthy, but even it has been affected by the rape. When the relationship was fairly new, I once again became very afraid of sex. I feared that if I had sex with this man, the relationship would become solely physical. I wanted to preserve the wonderful friendship we had established up to that point and feared that it would be lost once we had sex. If this happened, I would once again feel as though a man only wanted to be involved with me because of sex. By discussing our feelings openly and honestly and really communicating through every step, we were able to let our affection blossom into a beautiful relationship in which I am loved and accepted for who I am. In turn, I have for the first time been truly able to love, trust, and believe a man. I now view sex as a complement to the relationship, not as the focus or ulterior motive.

It is now going on twelve years since I was raped. Only by

dealing with the emotions of the experience through therapy, and with a great deal of determination and a desire to change, have I come to realize how much the rape has indeed affected my life, and how much I have survived.

A few years ago, for the first time in many years, I found that I accept and love myself for who I am. I now trust others as well as myself and my own judgment. I continue to work at expressing my feelings, knowing myself, and believing in who I am. Not only have I taken back the self-esteem I lost (and have actually achieved a higher level than before), but I have also put time, energy, and effort into mastering other parts of my life as well, and see myself becoming stronger, healthier, happier, and more conscious than ever before. I realize that I can be a victim again, but it will never have the same effects on me, because *no one* can take away who I am now.

12

Tears over
Black and Blue

❨

Lift up your faces, you have a
    piercing need
For this bright morning dawning
    for you.
History, despite its wrenching pain,
Cannot be unlived, but if faced
With courage, need not be lived
    again.

Lift up your eyes
Upon this day breaking for you.
Give birth again
To the dream.
Women, children, men,
Take it into the palms of your
    hands,
Mold it into the shape of your most
Private need. Sculpt it into
The image of your most public self.
Lift up your hearts
Each new hour holds new chances
For a new beginning.
Do not be wedded forever
To fear, yoked eternally
To brutishness.
The horizon leans forward,
Offering you space
To place new steps of change.

From On the Pulse of Morning
Maya Angelou

Leslie was twenty-five when it happened. That was twelve years ago, just a few months after she graduated from college.

One night after I had met my mother and brothers at The Improv in downtown Los Angeles, comedy turned to tragedy when my car radiator needed water. I was on my way home to Long Beach, but I didn't make it there that night. There was no water at the dark gas station I found, and I thought nothing of the two black men using the phone next to me. No one I called was home, just like earlier that day when I had tried to get one of my friends to come with me—a premonition.

———

The men grabbed me just before I got to my car and pushed me roughly into the passenger seat. I said, "Someone's coming for me," so they walked me to their large car and threw me in the back. They took turns driving and raping, and struck me across my eyes every so often, as though they were afraid I would remember what they looked like. I did what they said. I had no room for fear, as my whole focus was on survival. They smelled terrible. The older one was telling the other one what to do, as if he were training him. Sometime after I had lost my sense of time and direction, they stopped and stood me up in an alley next to a building, as though I were a broken doll.

———

After they drove away, I walked out to the street and saw the neon lights of a small motel. The Vietnamese owner let me in to call my mom and to wait for her. My left eye was swollen shut over my contact lens, but I felt no pain.

My mom and I spent the night at the hospital in Long Beach. After the tests, we waited four hours for the police to come. The long interrogation gave me little assurance that the rapists would be found. Back home, I had the indescribable feeling of being happy to be alive. My mom, visiting from the Central Coast, stayed with me a few days longer than planned. (I recently learned that my mom's boss almost fired her for this, even though she had told him the reason. Fortunately his boss rectified the situation.)

Before the rape, I had never used a female gynecologist. I knew at that point it was important for me to switch over. I was treated immediately for gonorrhea. The doctor's nurses looked alarmed when she gave me a double dose of penicillin. It was such a shock to my system that I could barely walk to my mom's car, but I knew that it was important to be treated right away.

The next step was to drive to Los Angeles to pick up my car, which had been impounded. My brother drove my mother and me, since I still could not wear my contacts and my glasses were in my purse, which was found a few days later. The policeman at the counter pulled my file and said matter-of-factly, "That'll be seventy-five dollars." My mom made a fuss to no avail, and I'll never forget his remark about my ordeal: It's good for you.

Then I was silent . . . silent even though for weeks I told people I'd had a racquetball accident to explain my black-and-blue eyes . . . silent even though I was fired from my new job for not keeping up with my share of the workload.

I felt powerless, and for years was unaware of the anger and rage I carried.

Then came the trial of Rodney King, the black man beaten by white officers in Los Angeles. I was moved when I heard King's tearful plea in response to the violent aftermath of the trial in which the police officers were acquitted: Can't we get along? I realized that my rage was not so much toward the men who had raped me as toward the law enforcement and judicial systems that allow these crimes to occur and go unpunished. The

William Kennedy Smith trial also triggered my rage. I knew his chances of being convicted were slim. His attitude of triumph following the trial was disgusting to me.

The effects of my rape, especially fear, often catch me by surprise. One year after the rape, I ran off a bus in downtown Los Angeles when I noticed it was empty except for the driver, who was a black man. I was terrified, yet the event seemed unreal. Six years later I was leaving a movie theater alone, since my friends and I were all driving separately to the restaurant where we were meeting. I could see only one man in the parking lot, and he was black. Adrenaline flowed as I ran to my car, and I was hysterical when I got to the restaurant. "Why didn't you wait for me?!" I cried to my friends. I'm still afraid of being alone in the city at night, and I often feel apprehensive when I'm alone in a room with a strange man.

Many of the effects went unnoticed by me until the last few years. But in talking to supportive people, thinking back and seeing patterns, or wondering, Why did I respond that way?, the answer is often clear now.

I haven't had a comfortable relationship with a man since my assault. For six years I dated much less than before, and my only intimate relationship was short-lived. I was quite comfortable with the most recent man I dated until we grew intimate. Then I felt myself getting angry at him too often, and that scared me. Once, it seemed that without even speaking, we ignited each other's anger (his ex-wife had left him for another man). Shortly after that, I ran away from him. It was early on a Saturday morning, and we were waking together. His attitude was uncaring and I felt frightened. I quickly dressed and walked home. Although he followed me and I let him drive me the rest of the way, we didn't see each other after that.

I had attended a personal growth workshop while in that relationship. In the first session, we each picked slips of paper with the names of emotions written on them that we were supposed to express. I picked *rage* and had difficulty summoning up this emotion. The facilitator told me to think of something in my life that had caused this, and I thought of the rape. Feeling the heat rise, I picked up a pillow and threw it against the wall with all of my might, completely surprised at my outburst. In the following sessions, I learned to express and release this anger by beating my fists into pillows. At home, I would slap the water in the bathtub, often so hard that the water dripped from the ceiling.

The director of the workshop had recommended a psychiatrist, and I began to meet with him shortly after leaving the relationship. He explained that until I could heal my repressed anger, I would continue to attract men who have their own anger.

While I'll never know just how much influence the rape has had on my life, it does seem subconsciously to cause me to maintain a certain separation from others that locks away my power and hides the key.

In the workplace, I have often been frustrated with not having enough responsibility or not being able to use the full range of my skills. Several years ago, one of my supervisors asked me why I had settled for a position without much creativity. "What happened?" Only recently have I learned the answer. And though I find myself in job after job where I bend to another's dictates more than I care to, I resent being told what to do. I believe this to be partly a result of the rape. When I *am* presented with challenges and responsibility, the negative forces of fear, worry, and insecurity sometimes interfere. In one job where I was a manager, I was fired after a year and told that my attitude was one of the main reasons. This was a surprise to me—for the most part I had liked my job. But my fears must have come across as a bad attitude.

Slowly and gradually, I'm discovering ways of melting the ice that holds my talents and dreams frozen. I recently had a dream in which I was sliding on ice, and I decided to use this symbol in a personal ceremony for myself. I found photos of me as a happy child and placed them on my mantel. I wrote words such as *healing*, *transformation*, and *joy*, and placed them on the coffee table. Then I lit candles and placed three bowls of ice cubes on the hearth. I lit a small fire and fed it until the ice melted, all the while affirming my intentions.

The next morning, my supervisor told me she had to let me go. I was working as a receptionist and probably did not hide the fact that I was frustrated and unhappy. I felt relieved and immediately called an architect I knew about a drafting position.

I started the next day. Suddenly those words in the candlelight held new significance for me.

I remember the tears that fell from my bruised eyes so long ago, looking at my mom, both of us silent. It seemed that deep within I knew the pain of fear and despair to come. And yet, there was also the joy of knowing how precious life is.

13

The Threads of My Life

❝

This woman describes her rape as the crack from which she emerged to really experience the fullness of life. By scraping away old values, she was able to piece together a new life. Since the rape, almost fifteen years ago, she has completed her undergraduate degree, graduated from law school, and is now a practicing attorney. She is fifty years old.

I was recently called for jury duty. Not until that morning did I realize I could be faced with hearing a rape trial. When the judge (who I had appeared before on other occasions) read the introductory information, I knew the situation was so similar to my own that I could not make a rational decision about the defendant's innocence. I could not even stop shaking. By the time the judge asked for a show of hands of those who wanted to be excused, I could hardly compose myself. I asked to speak to him in private. Along with the attorneys and the clerk and a microphone we stepped into the hall, and I told them that I had been involved in a similar rape trial and could not be fair and impartial. The attorneys were happy to excuse me.

I didn't think I could go back to work that day, so I took a long walk with my husband, Ronald, the dearest man alive. During lunch, he bought me a symbol of courage and strength—a silver goddess charm. I wear it to remind myself of what I learned that day: My center of courage and strength as a rape survivor lies in being the force in my life, and my own consciousness is able to take a stand for what I believe. That day I felt more whole, having once again experienced the raw emotions left from the rape.

At one time I was one of the walking dead—dead to my own life. I *was* successfully existing, physically and financially. The days came and went, the years rolled by, things got done, I got promoted, the children were growing up. I had ambitions, wishes, and small pleasures. I might have even been happy most of the time. I was living a life, but it was not mine. It was my first husband's, my children's, my family's, my employer's, and my church's. I was well known in the community. I even made the front page a couple of months before the rape as the "Women's Flour Packing Champion."

One waits for a magic moment that will signal "the reason for living." Maybe I was seeking spiritual guidance, maybe love, maybe lack of stress, maybe beauty around me. Whatever it was, it was yet to be found, much less defined or described. It was a knowing that there must be more to life. More of what?

There was no one day when I made the decision to live. I could mark the beginning as the events that resulted in the rapist's conviction. This was a turning point in my experiencing my own strength and power.

Nothing ever happens by accident. There are no coincidences. We are responsible. I always keep the following quote in my purse.

> Until one is committed there is hesitancy, the chance to draw back, always ineffectiveness. Concerning all acts of initiative (and creation), there is one elementary truth, the ignorance of which kills countless ideas and splendid plans; that the moment one definitely commits oneself, the Providence moves too. All sorts of things occur to help one that would never otherwise have occurred. A whole stream of events issues from the decision, raising in one's favour all manner of unforeseen incidents and meetings and material assistance, which no man could have dreamt would have come his way. I have learned a deep respect for one of Goethe's couplets: "Whatever you can do, or dream you can, begin it. Boldness has genius, power, and magic in it."
>
> *The Scottish Himalayan Expedition*
> *W. H. Murray*

The choices we make every day show up in the person we are and will become. If we fail to confront painful or hurtful things and if we repress them and fail to take a stand, we will have an empty spot that will grow each time the opportunity arises. Eventually this empty spot will become a vacuum where no "life" can live. Life abhors a vacuum, so into that vacuum will pour self-doubt, self-effacement, loss of power, and unconsciousness.

What were the forces in my childhood that made me into what I am? My childhood was reasonably normal: dinner every night, allowances, homework, chores on Saturday, bath on Saturday night, church on Sunday. We had the basic nuclear family. I had a physically safe and secure childhood. While some of my memories of junior high are painful—my clothes not matching, my doubts about boys, the initiation into sex, the early marriage and child at fifteen—I was still safe and secure. I had just substituted my parents for a husband. But ultimately I believe that what makes a difference in my life is what I choose to do with the next minute, not why I make the choice.

Somewhere along the way, before the rape, I began asking: Is this all there is?—usually in reference to the love of my husband. I felt I was withering, choking without the breath of life, and sinking further into a hole of mediocrity. My husband couldn't face what I was going through or understand the changes in me. He did not understand that my needs, when they did not coincide with his, could be valid. The man I had counted on was not there when I needed him most. A few months after the rape trial, I had tried to talk him into letting me take a few months off from work because we were moving to another house. But he had found a house near an airport that would allow him to park his airplane there and needed my income to be able to buy it. It was not what I wanted, but I gave in, again.

About five months after the trial, on December twenty-eighth, I left my family. I walked. I have never returned to the role of full-time mother, wife, working mother, self-sacrificing female holding the family together. I had to find a safe place to rest and to find relief from the stress of "doing it all."

I look back and see that I was at my emotional wit's end, probably suffering from post-traumatic stress disorder related to the rape. My value system had collapsed. I was born in the forties, raised and married in the fifties, a housewife in the sixties, and a working mother in the seventies. I was a born-again Christian—spoke in tongues even, a believer in social conscience and the

Puritan work ethic, and a liberal-thinking Democrat. Sex was the cause of all that was wrong in my life: the mistreatment by teenage boys; painful childbirth and dirty diapers; unwanted advances by men; uncaring demands by my first husband. Sex was not a loving, satisfying, nurturing experience. It was rough, demanding, necessary, and always took too long, even if I did have orgasms.

After the trial, I did discover a supportive shoulder to cry on. When I left the house that night with my hastily packed things, I went to where a coworker, Ronald, was house-sitting and stayed with him. When I did not go home, the house of cards fell in. Within two weeks my husband had filed for divorce and child custody.

Ronald was loving, undemanding, caring, and allowed me to have just what I needed—someone to listen and ask clarifying questions. He supported my decisions and loved me unconditionally. I cried, I rested, I healed. I slowly gained perspective.

We talked about life and about values, and it was during this time that I realized I wanted to pursue my goal of becoming a lawyer. I set my feet on the path of getting into undergraduate school, quitting my job, and looking for a part-time situation.

Later, I would describe my direction as putting one foot in front of the other. I did what I needed to do each day to make my goal of law school a reality—it drove all of my choices. I was beginning to enjoy being the center of my life. I was making decisions and executing them—property settlements, moving, selecting a major.

For the next seven years, I kept my direction. Money was always just barely there. My mother helped. The course load I chose was always just enough to support the next phase, whether it was getting into law school or passing the bar exam. No more. No less. I paid child support and had financial aid as well as part-time jobs to keep it all together.

I also had the settlement on the lawsuit against the State for negligence in having paroled the rapist. This was my "fresh start" money. I am thankful that I was able to afford law school. The threads of my life: having the financial support to do what I wanted. There is never enough to be extravagant—at least not for any time—but there is enough to plan for things that are wanted.

I made it through law school and even passed the bar exam. I consciously had to tell myself that it was OK to leave behind the limitations that I had always accepted. I discovered that all I had to do was to put one foot in front of the other.

Once while climbing Mount Baker, I took this concept even further. The wind was howling, my pack was heavy, my feet and hands were numb until I frantically wiggled or moved them long enough to get some circulation going. Every step was an enormous effort. Why go on? "I am going to fall off the mountain" . . . "I can't do this" . . . "It's too hard" . . . "I'm tired" . . . "I hurt with every step." But I always seemed to be able to remember my training and to take another step. I was safe—roped up with all of the right gear. I was fit. I wanted to reach the top. I noticed that I was doing what I usually did—wanting to escape an uncomfortable situation by going to sleep or running away. My mind made up scenarios to match the feeling of how too much risk would end in harm—in this case, physical harm. I looked at that thought and decided there was no real danger, just the thoughts of danger. I don't remember thinking that if I turned back I would be quitting. I just remember that I knew all I had to do to reach my goal was to put one foot in front of the other. The thoughts of life-threatening danger receded and in their place were just body sensations. I watched as I made it to the top. This was not my first mountain, but the highest yet and the most difficult. I climbed Rainier, Glacier Peak, Mount Hood, and other minor peaks during the next few years. I completed several ten-kilometer runs and one minitriathlon, usually placing in my age group. The threads of my life keep repeating themselves in different scenarios: just do what needs to be done to get me where I know I want to go.

After passing the bar, the two areas of my life that required exploration were career and companionship. We never see it coming until it is over. In December of 1989, I was offered a job in bankruptcy that I had wanted for quite some time. In that same month, I received a phone call from Ronald. I had not seen him in seven years—our lives had taken different paths. We met for lunch on December twenty-eighth and then spent a weekend together. The emotional charge that we created was just as sweet as the first time we were together and remains that way to this day.

There is no way to describe the violation of my being, my body, my spirit, my space of time called "me" that happened when I was raped. Like any fragile event of life-shaping proportions, I grieve over what was lost: innocence, values, the woman I was. The grief is still there; the anger is still there; the fear of something similar is still there; the tears are still there too.

Steeling myself against future loss, I have armed myself with a good defense. My new value system has rejected the old: the role of mother and dutiful wife, the status of being the property of any man, and the need of having another man around all the time to protect me.

The threads that run through my life are now intricately woven together with the rape and its aftermath. As I look at my life, my greatest pain is my vulnerability and my greatest joy is the hard-won self-confidence with which I face that pain. I have watched as my old values dissolved, the sacrifice of preciously held illusions, but the awareness of having experienced that change has brought me a powerful sense of self. With that I reach for the future.

14

Innocence
Lost

❝

Every April, Jennifer becomes
"tense and easy to anger." She
heard about this project during
April and decided to channel
these emotions into telling her
story.

It was early morning on April seventeenth, fifteen years ago, when the truck approached. I was running away from home. When it reached me, the driver asked if I needed a ride. I accepted because there was a female passenger already in the cab.

He drove to the courthouse and the woman got out. He assured me that he would then proceed to my destination (a bus stop), but I said I would walk because it wasn't that far from where we were. I tried to open the door, but the handle did not work. (The other female had gotten out on the other side of the truck.) The next thing I knew, he was back in and the truck was moving.

He drove in the opposite direction of my stop. I remember thinking very clearly that he was going to hurt me, but I was paralyzed. After driving in the hills for a while, he started back toward where we had come from. I told him to please just leave me back where he had found me. He responded that he was going to teach me not to run away.

———————

At this point, we were going about fifty miles per hour down a hill. I then tried to open my door to jump, but he grabbed my wrist and hit me. He pulled behind a horse stable and grabbed me again. Of course I screamed and tried to fight, but he was much bigger and stronger than me. The next thing I remember clearly is being on my stomach, with him on top of me pulling my pants down. I also remember that I couldn't breathe that well. He then assaulted me with his hand, telling me he would kill me if I said anything or if I tried to get away when he got up. I told him I couldn't breathe. He got off of me and took my pants all the way off, and then assaulted me orally. He then took his pants down and made me feel him and perform oral sex on him, as he put it, "to get him ready." He then laid me back on the seat and tried to have intercourse. For some reason, either because I was a virgin or because of the position, he could not penetrate.

But I remember the pain as though he had. He asked me if I wanted to suck on "it" instead, as if I were a willing partner. I, of course, said "no," so he kept trying. He finally gave up after what seemed to be a lifetime, and he told me to get dressed. He then put me into the horse stables. I was instructed to wait there until he drove away. I think I waited twenty minutes.

———————

Of course I reported the attack to the police, but *that* only got me further victimization. Not only did they, in my opinion, botch the investigation, but they also gave out my name to the owners of the horse stables. These people happened to have a daughter that went to my school, and so within a week I was the talk of the town. They weren't talking about how I had done nothing wrong, they were saying that I was a slut. When you are fourteen and everyone is talking aloud about something very personal and traumatic as though you are to blame, you start to believe them.

Here it is fifteen years later. The stables have been replaced by a restaurant—one that I refuse to patronize. I'm terrified of horses. And even though I tell myself that I was not to blame, I'm still trying to convince myself of that very fact. I still feel dirty, even after showers. My husband has had to deal with it as well. On several occasions he has rolled over to hold me at night, only to have me jump out of bed yelling at him. The problem seems to be getting worse as time goes by.

Until recently, I was unable to talk about the rape to anyone, including my husband. He knew what happened, but he didn't *know*. Now, we do talk about it openly. I guess that's the only way I am ever really going to heal. But I can't seem to forget anything about the attack or my attacker. I can see his hands and face as clearly as I did fifteen years ago. And that is the most difficult part.

15

Looking For a Fix

❝

MARIA WRITES, "SUCCESS—THE
DISTANCE I HAVE TRAVELED SINCE
I CAME TO KNOW MYSELF."

Maria gives a detailed account of
the effects of having been sexually
abused as a child and raped sixteen years ago at the age of forty.
She talks about addictions, flashbacks, relationships, treatment,
and self-revelations.

I was raped by an acquaintance—he was the boyfriend of a friend. He was always flirting with me, and I did not like him and wondered what my friend could possibly see in him. He was everything that I disliked: unkempt, arrogant, pudgy, the type of man who looked at women as if he was undressing them. He worked for the federal government in a responsible position. The first time I saw him, I felt creepy. It was my intuition warning me to be careful. Unfortunately I ignored this feeling, as I always did at that time. I convinced myself that he must be OK because my friend was OK.

It is important for me to include a description of the person I was before the rape because it is so contrary to what I became after the rape. I was cheerful, bright, attractive, and on my way to reaching my aspirations. I had worked for the federal government since 1970 and managed to be promoted six times in five years. I felt very good about myself and was well within reaching my career goals. I had been seeing one man for about six months and was very happy with him. I was not looking for anyone else.

The rapist had asked me for dates and had invited me to go on trips. He told me that no one needed to know. I repeatedly told him no. The day I was raped, my partner was out of town. I had stopped at a bar close to work. Whenever I was overly tired from work, I would stop and have a drink or a Coke and let traffic settle down. That day, when I was ready to leave, the rapist offered to walk me to my car. I declined, and the owner of the bar said that he would walk me out instead. In the meantime, a customer came in, so I told the owner that this man could walk me to my car.

When we arrived, he tried to kiss me. I said no and pushed him away, believing it was settled. I unlocked my car and started to get in when he tried to kiss me again. I said, "Stop it!" He said, "Come on, Maria. You know you want it." I said, "The hell I do. Get the hell out of here!" He knocked me onto the front seat and started touching me. He pulled my panty hose down and off of one leg, and he raped me. It seemed like a year, but it only took a minute or so.

As soon as he finished, he left. I just lay there in shock. I felt dirty and violated. I blamed myself and felt that I had done something to provoke it. Now I know that this was not true. I did not ask for it, and I did nothing to lead him on. It was not my fault.

I did not call the police. I just wanted to keep it quiet, because I was sure that they would blame me and say that I had asked for it. In the seventies, more than today, the woman was always blamed. I wanted to survive and to continue in my job. I was sure that reporting it would ruin my career. When I awoke the next day, I felt as if I was in a nightmare one minute and in denial the next. I even called the rapist and do not know why. Maybe I wanted him to say that he would not tell anyone or that he was sorry for hurting me. He didn't.

I did not tell anyone. I went on, building on my pain and anger and becoming more and more depressed. My boyfriend and I broke up within a couple of months because I allowed what had happened to come between us. He kept after me to find out what was wrong, and I drove him away with my actions. Little by little, what normalcy I had in my life turned to insanity. My behavior changed radically; I was constantly depressed. My drinking and intake of prescription drugs picked up. I needed a fix for my pain, and I could not find a permanent one.

I used men as objects to satisfy myself. One man that had been pursuing me talked me into going out, and of course we had sex. Afterward, he told me that he had felt as if *he* had been raped. I would have sex and then hate myself for my weakness of "sleeping around." My taste in men changed from decent, loving, caring, affectionate, intimate men to heavy drinkers. The relationships I had were impersonal and empty.

I eventually lost all of my friends. I no longer valued relationships and came to believe that no one would stay and that all relationships were temporary. I isolated myself. I desperately wanted someone to love me but could not love and respect myself. If I met someone nice, I would find something wrong with him because I felt unworthy of love and happiness. I gave double messages—I would say that I wanted a relationship and, at the same time, I would push the man away. Several men who cared about me told me that I would not let anyone get close to me, so that they might be able to love and know me.

I made a point of punishing the white men I dated because the rapist was white. Eventually I ended up going to bars alone and picking up men and hating myself in the morning. I would tell myself that I would never do it again. Ultimately, I did, and the vicious cycle of regrets and self-hatred continued. I was really down on myself because of my behavior—it was so atrocious—but I had no control over it.

I hated myself so much that I could not look in the mirror. I never smiled at myself. I would make up my face and look at a portion of it—never the whole face. My lips drooped in a constant frown. Smiling was difficult for me, as if it would hurt my face.

I had never been able to tolerate people who tried to control me. After the rape, this became an obsession. I always had to be in control personally and professionally. I was either abrasive or manipulative. I loved my job as an equal rights specialist because it enabled me to go after perpetrators, but eventually I had to leave that profession because I just burned out. I still worked hard but never got the promotions to go with it. I always felt like a victim, and my self-worth continued to plummet.

My relationship with my daughter worsened after the rape. I

took my anger and pain out on her, and she and I have suffered terribly for it. She's now married to a fine man and has two children, but I worry about her because of what she inherited from me. The pain that I didn't work out was passed onto her. I believe that with rape as well as with dysfunctions such as alcoholism, the results are multigenerational—my behavior affected her feelings, actions, and choices, as hers will affect those of her children.

Six years after the rape, I was in Washington, D.C., on business. The rapist heard through colleagues that I was there and showed up at my hotel. My hate and anger were still so repressed that I conversed with him as if the rape had not occurred. In fact, I did not truly accept how much I hated him until recently, sixteen years after the rape. I still have periods of hating myself for not telling anyone what happened to me. Just telling one person would have lifted the burden and alleviated my anger.

I met my match on controlling by manipulation when I became involved with a married alcoholic. One night both of us got a DUI and spent the night in jail. He chewed me up and spit me out. He was like a drug of choice to me. I kept thinking that I could make him change, but it never happened. I finally had to wean myself away from him a little at a time. I succeeded, but in the meantime, the relationship had devastated me. I was drinking heavier and smoking marijuana in addition to taking prescription drugs.

Then I punished myself by depriving myself of male company, relationships, and sex. I could not stand to touch myself because the self-hatred was eating me up.

My life continued like this until five years ago, when I went into treatment for alcoholism. I was very depressed and angry all the time. Everything was falling apart. When I started looking into my alcoholism and my drug dependency, I found that there was something deeper there—they were the symptoms, not the real problems. Each time that I did the Fourth Step—a written moral inventory—at Alcoholics Anonymous, I found out more about myself. But I kept hurting . . . people were getting well around me . . . and I still had problems.

When Marilyn Van Derbur Atler, Miss America of 1958, came out in May 1991 and said that she had been sexually abused by her millionaire father, I knew that something like that had happened to me. I *finally* consciously remembered the rape and a couple of childhood experiences of sexual abuse. I went to the Kempe Center for the Prevention and Treatment of Child Abuse and Neglect, and I also went to WINGS, a support group for incest survivors. Through them, I started finding out more about myself, and that is when I started having flashbacks. I remembered the rape, felt my emotions, and realized the enormity of its effects on my life.

It takes guts to look at sexual abuse. Flashbacks are very painful. You need to feel the emotions you stuffed so that you begin healing. You cannot heal with knowledge alone: *You can only heal by feeling.* Sometimes it seems like the feelings are going to kill you. Sometime ago, I kept having the same extremely painful flashbacks, and it seemed more than I could bear. At one point I asked my therapist, "Did these things really happen to me?!" Then I went into denial and stopped feeling. I turned off the emotions and the memory of what had happened because they were just too painful. After several days a tear trickled out of my eye. I thanked God for that tear because I knew that I was able to feel again.

I am glad that things have changed so that women can come out and say that they were raped. From the time that I was a little girl I learned not to tell anyone anything. This was my defense mechanism for many years.

I am still paying for the choices that I made since I was raped. I have not remarried. My career went downhill. I never got a promotion after the rape, although I had jobs with promotion potential. I set myself up for failure. I always wondered why I lost all of my motivation and could not succeed. Now I know: My whole life changed because of a man's need for violence and control. The most painful part for me is to realize how much the man affected my life *in one minute of violence.* I feel that he actually had control of my life for sixteen years because my unresolved anger and rage took on a life of its own. I unconsciously gave him power over my life. I hope that because I have changed my behavior and because my daughter now understands what happened we can make it better for her children.

There are times that I still feel deep hatred and revulsion toward him. I wish every bad thing that can happen to a human being would happen to him for violating me. He stole from me and my future, and for that I have wished him the worst of all there is in every aspect of his life. I've thought he is the lowest of human beings and deserves no compassion or goodness. I hope to be able to let go and stop giving him so much time in my head. I am in therapy to help me do this. I will never know what I could have been if he had not raped me. I will never know how much happiness I missed with my daughter, mother, sisters, and friends.

I do know there will be a time to let go, but for now I still find myself wanting desperately to turn back the clock, as if it had never happened. But now that I know what happened, it's my responsibility to stop it from affecting my life today. I have to live with and accept the reality of it.

Recovery is really something. I find myself at a fork in the road: One choice leads me down the familiar easy path that involves old ideas and behaviors. The other path is the one I choose consciously now. It involves using the new behaviors I have learned in recovery—facing the unknown and taking risks in order to have new experiences. I now make choices with my wisdom and consciousness instead of with my pain and confusion. I am learning to express anger without rage, and, slowly, I am accepting the fact that my life took a totally different turn as a result of the rapist's violence. Instead of looking for an artificial fix, though, the only fix for my pain comes from within. I am fifty-six years old, and I am glad for this. What I have left of the life that God has blessed me with will be happier. I won't be burdened by this garbage that I did not know was bothering me.

One of the biggest changes in my life is that I no longer feel like a victim. I work very hard at having appropriate boundaries between myself and others and evaluating who can be trusted. I am no longer as hard on myself and am very aware of my inner child and the need to nurture myself. Since I have been in therapy, much of the pain and anger has been resolved. I don't even know if I am an alcoholic anymore. The alcohol had just been a way to cover up all of my pain. I see a new happy person emerging out of that pain and confusion. I am grateful for the way my life is today, and I am really looking forward to my future.

Just prior to publication, Maria reviewed her story, which she had written fifteen months earlier. Her addendum:

I really felt as if I was reading the story of someone else instead of my own. I read it without regret, anger, or hate. Initially I experienced a deep sadness for the suffering and pain of this woman who was me and then acceptance that the deepest suffering is over. There is a hymn that is played at church called "All Is Well with My Soul." When they play it, I am very thankful that I now know what it is like to have contentment. All I need to do now is to live my life to the best of my ability one day at a time.

Psalm 131:2 "Surely I have calmed and quieted my soul, like a weaned child with his mother; like a weaned child is my soul within me."

16

Lookin' at the Past in the Rearview Mirror

❨

KAY WRITES, "I THINK THAT ANA-
LYZING IS REALLY GOOD, BUT
WHEN I START ANALYZING MY
ANALYZATIONS, THAT IS WHEN I
REALLY THINK I'M CRAZY."

Kay believes that one of the really positive results of the publicity about date rape in the past few years is that date rape is now a term everybody knows. Seventeen years ago, when she was sixteen, it didn't occur to her that she had been raped. She knew she didn't want it to happen, and she knows nobody would have called it rape.

always felt as if I had been born into the wrong family. As were most people in my small Midwestern town, my family was conservative. I considered myself to be liberal, so I never fit in with them. Part of my teenage rebellion was dating an older guy with a motorcycle who was not the kind of person a naive young lady should be hanging around. We had plans to run away to Florida together. One day he raped me in his apartment. I was sixteen years old, and this was my very first sexual experience. It never occurred to me that I had the right to say no. And it also never occurred to me that being forced to submit sexually was *not* normal. I think I simply believed that I had put myself in that situation and that I would get out OK if I was "cool" about it. About a week later, I took my small life savings out of the bank, split it with this guy, and made plans to meet him in Florida. I got down there and called him, only to discover that the number was nonexistent. He had deceived me. It did not occur to me to return home. I had looked at my hometown when I left and said to myself that it was the last time I'd be seeing it. I had run away for good.

The people who you fall in with as a runaway in a Greyhound bus station in the middle of the night are not desirable types. I met a man who said he would help take care of me. He took me to another man in a stinking little trailer out in the middle of nowhere for the purpose, I believe now, of selling me.

This was probably the worst experience that I had. They got me drunk and drugged. The only thing I could remember was that the light of day changed twice, so I think I was there for two or three days. It was a constant rape, every position possible. I don't think I fought it because it seemed useless—being in the middle of nowhere with two men. It was a horrific experience; I repressed the memory of it for a number of years. The full implications of what had happened did not occur to me until a couple of years ago when I realized that I could have been sold into slavery. I think that happens more than society realizes. For some reason I was not sold, and the guy drove me back to a town.

———

I hooked up with some people who were going to California and traveled there with them. I met a very nice man who I lived with until he discovered I was only sixteen. He was the first good man I had ever met. He put me in a boardinghouse and paid the first month's rent. At that time I felt more in control of things. I was working as a hotel maid, making barely enough money to live on. It was a meager existence, but at least I was not living on the streets.

This was when, for most of my life, I thought the first rape occurred.

———

He had followed me from the bus stop. The boardinghouse had a rule that men were not allowed inside. When I woke up and realized this man had broken into my room and that I was being raped, "No men allowed" was the first thought in my mind. I didn't scream because I did not want to be thrown out onto the streets.

———

Once again, the mind-set—I will survive if I can just hold on until it is over—kicked in. I was always operating with this attitude—if I just deal with it for right now, it will be over. I believed that because I ran away from home, it was my fault that these things were happening. I didn't have time to be upset. Maybe some rich person had time to be upset and go to therapy, but I didn't. I had to survive there and then. I just stuffed it all in the back of my brain.

From my teenage years to my midtwenties, I became dependent on dysfunctional men. I lived with an alcoholic, a coke addict, even someone who was living under an alias.

Eventually, I took Model Mugging. That changed a lot of things for me, because, for the first time, I saw all of those initial sexual experiences as rapes. Instead of the boardinghouse experience being the first rape, I realized the one in the biker's apartment was. In Model Mugging, I learned to "say no to the things that hold you back." I started to do that. It was no longer OK that my present husband was spending all of our money on coke.

This was also the time that I started to experience a deeper sexual awareness. Up to this point, sex had been interesting and exciting in the very beginning of the relationship, but I soon lost interest once the relationship developed. I had subconsciously learned to use sex as a way to survive when I was young. After taking Model Mugging, I became vocal when I did not want to be sexual.

Shortly thereafter, I returned to the Midwest to nurse my mother, who was terminally ill. The process of caring for her at this point in her life really brought our relationship full circle. At this time I also met Jerry, my mother's neighbor, who visited her every day when she was dying; he visited her more than her own relatives did. When our relationship started, it was just like all the other ones—sex was exciting and fun in the beginning, but I became disinterested once we started living together. He is intelligent and sensitive enough that he was able to piece things together. I see now that because of all the rapes, I had built a brick wall around myself (complete with a piranha-infested moat) in terms of letting any men in. Maybe I'm fearful of letting someone in that close.

Control and trust are the two big issues that I am working on now. If I am in control of everything in my sphere—my house, my emotions, my interactions, and my love for other people—then life is good. Sex in a fulfilling relationship really epitomizes loss of control. That has held me back. I feel like I have frequently put myself in a position in which the man I was involved with was more in love with me than I was with him. Therefore, in my mind, I have the upper hand in The Control Game. It goes back to being hurt physically and emotionally over and over again.

In general, I am hypersensitive to the interactions between women and men. I can be sitting next to a couple and develop a whole scenario in my mind about the way that the "schmuck" is treating her. I carry those things with me. I'm very sensitive to common misogyny; it really upsets me. I work in a male-dominated industry. My male co-workers say things that make me grit my teeth. They don't have a clue. Then, I think I'm crazy or way too sensitive. I'll tell myself to lighten up. Other people have their faults and who am I to judge them? Then I go back to believing that while our society has changed in the past twenty years, we still have a long, long way to go.

If only there were more men like Jerry who are kind and intelligent. I am so distrusting of all men, but I don't want to be that way. I don't know what else to do with my feelings. Just when I think that I am doing well, then something happens to set me off. I saw an ad for a movie that showed a woman with her hands and feet tied and a man standing above her. That sets me off because I have been tied up . . . and raped. Why are they watching it for entertainment? I have a difficult time understanding why anyone would willingly go to a movie that shows violence against women.

I went into therapy for a short time when I started having flashbacks. I had no idea when the flashbacks would hit, and, of course, they came at the most inopportune times. I am resistant to returning to therapy at this time, even though I might benefit from it, because I am so tired of dealing with "it." I need to turn around and see these issues as part of my past. I want to transform "objects in mirror are closer than they appear" to "objects in mirror are fading fast."

I have experienced total anguish over my attitude toward sex. I wish that thinking about it and knowing about it made a difference, but they don't. I understand why I'm not interested in sex, but that doesn't change it. I want to *want to* have sex, because I have someone who I love very dearly. So often I apologize to him. I have been cheated out of a birthright, something that should be savored and enjoyed. Now I want it back. I hope that my new mind-set of thinking of these things as part of my past will help. Thank god I have an open mind. Sometimes I wonder if it will ever be over. I want to live a full and rich life. I'm almost there. I have most of the things that are really important in life. Maybe in a year I'll have a baby. I want to spend my life having fun. I'm tired of dealing with this.

I really credit Jerry with giving me the opportunity to talk about a lot of things. If it weren't for him, I don't think I would be where I am now. In my past relationships, I always viewed the breakdown of the sexual aspect as a function of the men being jerks. Whereas in this relationship that isn't the case. It was very difficult for me to admit that the problem with sex stemmed from all I had been through, even though I knew it in my heart. Sometimes I feel that what I really need is to get back to my women friends. We really grew up together and they have been through some of this. From the time I was twenty to twenty-eight, I was in almost constant contact with them. In the past four years, I have moved four times, so it is difficult to maintain strong ties. I feel that if I could be around them, I could talk to them and be understood.

Sometimes I try to imagine how anybody could rape another person. I have tried to live my life so that I do unto others as I would have them do unto me. I don't think a man can possibly know what it is like to be vulnerable unless something has happened to render him defenseless. If they knew what it was like, I don't think that they would want to hurt others.

I feel like all of life's experiences have a purpose. Even as I was going through all of the bad times, I always felt that I had an angel on my shoulder. There has got to be a purpose for me going through hell when I was so young. The only one that I can identify is that now it's my turn to help other people who are in need. I most closely identify with runaways. They run away for a reason. And if they are on the streets, then they are being victimized all over again because that is the way of the street. I feel that one of the things I want to do in my life is to establish a place for runaways, a place where they can go to sleep without being hassled. That is one of the daily concerns of runaways: Where am I going to sleep?

I wonder about the people who raped me. If everything happens for a reason, what was the reason that they were doing such horrible things to me? I survived for a reason, but what was the purpose of *them* doing it to me? People have told me that I am being too generous with these folks to think that there is a reason why I was there. I don't really know how else to look at it.

Do I have to feel rage in order to heal? I have never felt it, though I have tried to. I am mad that those people took something away from me, but I don't *feel* rage.

For a long time, I thought that I was really assertive because I knew that I never wanted to be raped again. I found out after an incident, however, that I wasn't as assertive as I had thought. I had an old car with a leak in the radiator and always had to fill it up. Once, at a service station, a guy walked up behind me and asked if he could help. I figured he was just a condescending attendant and told him that I did this every night, that I didn't need any help. He insisted that I let him help me, however, and started to reach out with his hand. I turned around to tell him again that I didn't need any help. Instead of a gas station attendant, it was some guy in jeans and a Hawaiian shirt with his dick hanging out, and he was flopping it at me. I stood there, and my only response was, "Uungh, uungh, uungh. . . ." He laughed and said he was sorry. Then I got really pissed that he said he was sorry, because this asshole obviously knew better. So I grabbed him by the collar and sprayed water all over him, cussing him out. He stumbled away, and I was left standing there, pissed as hell for what he had done. Two men walked by and asked me if I was OK. I told them what the guy had done and they repeated, "But are you OK?" Of course I was OK, but I was madder than hell.

My first reaction had been one of paralysis, and I knew that I had to change that. My second reaction was one of total disbelief. If that jerk had been violent, neither of those reactions would have saved me. It was at that time that I signed up for Model Mugging. I feel really sorry for the first guy who ever crosses me now because I'm not sure if I'll ever be able to stop. I have this feeling that all of the anger and rage I have that I can't seem to find now will come out then.

I really am an optimist, so I often wonder about when we as a society are going to stop abusing people. It does not seem to be human nature to hurt one another. It is very difficult for an optimist to come to terms with this. I have been hurt, but I don't think that I have been really hurt. I have never been broken up over the end of a relationship. I started them and I ended them. My heart has never been broken. It has been stepped on and tossed around, but I have never let people in enough to have them break it. I think it is time now to open it up. It just needs to happen. To talk about it is good.

17

Pure Potential

☾

TONI WRITES, "IF YOU CAN SUR-
VIVE RAPE, YOU CAN SURVIVE
ANYTHING."

Toni is currently a cofacilitator for a sexual assault survivors group. She is completing her associate's degree in human services and plans to work toward a master's degree in transpersonal psychology. She is a single mother of four and an aspiring artist. Her creativity in the art of shield making has played an integral part in her healing process and has served her in becoming, once again, spiritually connected. Her life has become enriched, full of possibilities and hope.

I grew up in what is now called a dysfunctional family system. I suppose that it was my legacy in life to continue the cycle of abuse that I had come to know so well. It has taken me half my life to learn how to smash this cycle—not only for myself, but for my children as well.

My name is Toni and I am a survivor. I wasn't always a survivor—once I was a victim. Before that, I was just a child—that is until that summer night eighteen years ago, the night five young men carried me up the stairs. Up to that point it was a game. I had no cause to fear them—three were friends of mine.

I was thirteen years old and I stopped enjoying the game when they held me down across the bed and removed my clothes. One by one they took their turns with me. Later, I heard it referred to as "pulling a train" on me.

I remember little about the act itself. I recall, instead, the laughter. There were five women in the hall, watching through the doorway, and they were laughing at me and at this thing that was being done to me.

Those young men stole more than just my virginity. They took my innocence and self-respect. They twisted who I was and left me confused, betrayed, and damaged. I became different. I felt I no longer belonged anywhere. Life as I knew it was over for me, and most of what was taken from me could never be replaced.

My encounter with the "wheels of justice" left me powerless and afraid. Somehow I was the criminal. I recall being placed in a chair by a bald, red-faced, angry man. He hooked me up to a machine that would prove not that I was telling the truth, but that I was lying. He was yelling at me, his questions assaulting me. I was terrified of him. He stomped out of the room and informed my parents that I was a liar.

What happened to me went unpunished. Thus it was condoned and somehow I was to blame. I began to confuse sex and love. This fit in neatly with the confusion of violence and love that I knew within the walls of my own home. The response of the community and the law enforcement agency only served to perpetuate the cycle of violence in my life.

I became promiscuous. This promiscuity was not based on a need or a desire for sex, but for love. I believed *sex was love.* I suppose that what I did was to reenact continually the shame that ultimately claimed who I had become. My quest for "love" was endless, painful, and humiliating. With my self-respect stolen and my self-esteem beaten beyond recognition, it seemed as if I had no "self" at all, except what others afforded me. It's not surprising then, that at the age of fifteen, I was again raped.

I remember that I knew what was going to happen. I cried, but they were silent tears. I asked a God I thought unjust, Why? Was once not enough? But this time was different—this man played no game with me. Survival was crucial. I assessed everything carefully, my mind alert and crystal clear. I noted his knife and his mood swings. I took in the scene with sharp clarity—the make of the car, the brand of his cigarettes, the color of his lighter, the odd gearshift and the tilted front end—anything and everything. How I walked away from this one haunts me still.

I had to choose the worst kinds of humiliation for myself. Much later I learned that I "chose rape," and in so doing, chose survival. After he raped me the first time, I could hear voices drifting through the forest. If I could just get to them somehow, I would be safe. After another "round" in the backseat, I explained that I had to go to the bathroom. It was my intention to run toward the voices, to be seen or to be heard. But he was alert because of my earlier attempt to get his knife. He stepped outside ahead of me, and I found that I had no choice but to squat before him and urinate. The humiliation was almost enough to kill me but was not stronger than my will to survive. Back into the car for another round. My mind raced. Instinctively I knew he was going to kill me when he was finished. It was in his ravings as well as in his moments of lucidity. This was no game. The humiliation continued. I feigned the exhausted lover. I praised his "lovemaking" abilities. I said that I was so tired, could we please stop now? He seemed to hesitate, and he soon fell into my web. He spilled out stories of his failing marriage, his wife's nagging and lack of empathy for him. He rambled on and on as I played amateur therapist. Somehow I managed to slip in that it was nearing my curfew and that I must get home or I would get in trouble. He started up the car and asked for directions. I got him to the hill above my house. As I opened the door he reached over and pulled it shut. He looked at me suspiciously. He verbalized his doubts in allowing me to go free. My heart stopped. Moments became hours. I said some things that today I cannot recall. I said them calmly, as if my heart, which was slamming in my chest, was still. I stepped out of the car. I took a step, slowly, calmly, then another. Then I bolted down the hill as fast as my young legs would carry me until I was home and safe. Safe, and yet tormented by my choices for survival. Today I work to honor these choices.

The system, once again, tried to find me responsible for the acts of violence committed against me. This time though a young detective was assigned to my case. He was like a knight in shining armor to me. He was kind and gentle with me, and careful. He told me that he believed me. To make things easier, he showed me a photo of the rapist because identification was only a formality at this point. (I knew the man's name by the end of the ordeal.) It was when I went before the grand jury that things fell apart again. They asked me if I had seen a lineup. I said that I had seen a photograph. They verified my answer, and all hell broke loose. I was supposed to have seen an official lineup. It was a violation of the "rules." The rapist was never prosecuted.

My promiscuous days were over then. I believed that it was my promiscuity that led to the rape. Perhaps the little white-haired man on the grand jury assisted in this conclusion. He tormented me with questions about my sexual experiences and behaviors, as if that would explain the whole situation and we could all go home and stop wasting everyone's precious time. The truth is I *was* promiscuous. So I went full swing in the other direction and got married. I longed for love and goodness, and marriage seemed logical to my dysfunctional mind. Abuse seemed normal to me as well.

The roles of victim and survivor were deeply rooted within me. The victim in me chose an abusive husband and the survivor in me chose to end the relationship. Because I knew nothing of healthy love or relationships, violence had become the acceptable form of communication for me. And yet, that child inside of me who needed love so badly assumed that if I loved a man enough, he would love me back. Basically, I tried to fix men. I loved them but received unending anger and violence in return. I did not know about breaking patterns; instead, I continued the patterns, over and over, through five marriages.

My fourth husband had a brother who was in prison for brutally raping a young girl. Ever the rescuer and savior of lost souls (except for my own), I felt that if we supported him, perhaps he would not rape again. I encouraged my husband to contact his brother.

Very soon my husband's brother began calling when he knew my husband was not at home. One night he said, "So he finally told you the truth. It's about time!" I had no idea what he was talking about and said so. He went on to explain that it was his duty to inform me that they *both* had participated in the rape. The victim could not tell them apart, and so my husband had not been charged. I was devastated. We had been married only two weeks. I filed for divorce immediately. I could not believe the deception, that this man I had known and loved was a rapist!

His brother continued to call after all of this. He expressed compassion and concern for me. We grew close, through the mail and on the phone. He showed me in countless ways how remorseful and reformed he was. In my grief, I chose to lean on him. Upon his release, we were married within a week. It was the ultimate closure. Not only would I love the rapist, I would prove that I was OK by marrying him as well.

The bruises he inflicted were quickly reported by concerned friends. But this was an intelligent man and I soon learned a new game—psychological battering. He made me feel as if everything was my fault. My identity was held hostage. He took from me until there was nothing left.

It was then that I attempted to take my own life. Death looked like the only way out for me. I could not seem to leave him any other way. You see, it wasn't *him,* it was *me*—I understood this with great clarity. It was a belief he worked hard to instill in me. That is the result of the fine art of "crazy making." It all became my fault.

The slashing of my wrist was no small thing. It required five hours of microscopic surgery to repair. Almost two years later, my hand still does not function properly. Yet it was then that something shifted for me. The survivor within was rearing its head again. I began to rage. And I could *feel* once again. Even though the emotion was anger, it was a sign that I was still in there somewhere. He used my rage to further his game. He labeled me "psycho bitch" and began a new campaign to convince my friends and my family that I was indeed crazy.

It was then that I met Bruce. He dealt in anger management and I chose to see him—ironically—because my husband had convinced me that I should. But Bruce's expertise did not end with anger issues. He also specialized in battered woman's syndrome and sexual assault issues. Somehow he got through to the pathetic mess I had become. Bruce taught me the fine art of "self-care." He taught me about boundaries and how to say no. He showed me how to rely upon myself, not others. He showed me how I might meet my own needs, and that I am responsible for my own choices and behaviors, and no one else's. With this comes the further responsibility of never harming others in the course of meeting those needs. If we speak from our hearts and stand in our truth, we will all be OK. He handed something to me, and one day, I saw that it was me.

Life's circumstances, no matter how devastating, can become a vehicle toward growth and inner healing. My life is changed now and I see myself as pure potential.

I continue into my second year of therapy. I have committed myself to the martial arts as a way of channeling the energy long stored up inside of me. I have taken steps toward finishing an education that I began ten years ago. I am learning how to apply my experiences in ways that may influence change in others and in society.

But there is a price for all this, it seems: the need for locks on my doors; looking over my shoulder; alertness to the possibility of danger—the shadow who is my ex-husband; most important of all—the effects on my children. Have I broken the cycle for them? Or was I too late?

Probably the last remaining consequence of my experiences with rape is the rage that I feel inside of me. It is rage at the injustice that people like myself have been made to suffer. My rage is directed toward society at all levels: the ones who blame the victim or who simply do not believe; the justice system, which rarely works to afford us protection or appropriate prosecution; a rehabilitation system that is far from effective, or, in the absence of rehabilitation, a system that merely warehouses perpe-trators. In this state, where violent rape occurs at twice the national average, I want to know, *Where is the outrage?*

I have come a long way, and I have a long way still to go. But I have reclaimed my sense of self. I possess the strength and courage of the inner Warrior. We who have survived rape owe it to ourselves to see that this is what we are—Warriors and Sisters. It is through this inner strength and courage that we continue to survive the label of "victim." Through sheer grit and staying power we learn to take back what was stolen from us. Today, I have goals and dreams. Best of all, I have worth and value as a human being.

The cost for this was high. The injustice is that these things were my birthright until they were taken from me eighteen years ago. And in spite of all that I have gained since that summer night, I cannot seem to stop the laughter in the hallway. There are scars that fade but do not disappear. Yet, we should choose to see these scars as living proof of who we are—survivors, Warriors, and anything else we choose to become—because *we are* pure potential. And the very substance that lives within us and told us we would survive is the very substance that will see us heal. Believe.

18

A Rape and Its Aftermath

❨

Pat Scott

Pat writes, "I'd say that the history of assault and battery against women has created an environment similar to war—wondering when the enemy will strike, wondering if you're prepared, wondering how much of your life to dedicate to defense, wondering mostly how to continue to live in spite of such fear. How to continue to live in spite of fear is perhaps the most glaring question that remains after being raped. I'm a forty-four-year-old female survivor of a rape that occurred almost twenty years ago. I remember thinking at the time, My life will be changed forever from this. I was right."

I don't remember the date. It was about twenty years ago. Indeed, many of the most noteworthy things in life go unrecorded in my journal. I'm too caught up in the events themselves or unable to find words to chronicle them. With rape, however, reliving it in any way—memory or print—is acid etching upon the soul.

I don't "remember it as though it was yesterday." Instead, like most memories, there are mismatched bits and snaggle-edged pieces.

———

I remember carrying groceries from my car to the door of my ugly little rental house—unkempt, overgrown, uncared for. I fumbled with the lock and opened the door. I sensed a "wrongness" and stayed outside wondering what to do. Should I leave and call the police? But they wouldn't come; there had been no crime. Call a friend? And jeopardize a life or look the fool. But if I left, simply closing the door against someone in my house, would an intruder be gone when I returned?

There were and are no answers, only questions. Why wasn't my dog barking to greet me? Where was my cat to welcome me? And what did I leave behind the door, obstructing it from opening completely?

The man behind the door wore a stocking mask. His face was distorted, impossible to identify and terrifyingly inhuman. He was nervous, excited, someone to beware of. He smelled of sweat, and he muttered disjointedly. Against my throat a gun was alien and cold. Later, against my heart, I saw it was square—a shiny silver semiautomatic.

It becomes fragmented here.

I remember offering money; he took it, smiled, and didn't leave. I asked if he had a girlfriend; he did. I remember he told me to pretend to enjoy it, and I thought, This is the same act friends find pleasure in. I remember praying to remnants of sixteen years of Catholic education—my statue of the Blessed Mother and a print of Dali's *Crucifixion of St. John on the Cross*.

I was lucky, in a sense. I wasn't beaten or tortured, and it didn't last for days. I told the intruder my (nonexistent) boyfriend was expected home soon and a business associate might be dropping over. He had me drive us to his friend's house, where I refused to get out. One man, one gun, one quick death was better than two or more violators and a slow dying. Confused, the guy had me drop him off on a corner and "not look back." I fled.

―――――――

I called my best friend for help. As I drove into the city, "The Way We Were" played on the radio. It reminded me that I had become just another dull rape statistic while my life was changed forever. Time to come would be measured against this point.

It's fairly painless to talk about the actual events of the rape. The words come out pale and arid—as devoid of emotion as William F. Buckley discussing Tweedledum and Tweedledee—a tale about something not very important by someone who wasn't there. But it is important and I was there. I just don't want to go back, I suppose.

Talk about the aftermath and my mind becomes a trembling and strident fountain, spewing twenty years of atrocities perpetuated by human beings upon other humans. Headlines scream of the tortured death of another woman victim. Without even reading the gory details, I shake and rage and cry, get headaches and lose sleep—a kind of post-traumatic stress disorder. My mind doesn't relive it in words and pictures, but the imprint on my body never leaves—shakes, sweat, numbing fear, dry mouth, a loosened bowel muscle. Perhaps it's because suddenly I'm confronted by a fabric woven of strands incomparably strong and unconscionably inhuman. It's life, and the dark force is winning.

The aftermath includes a mental tape containing all the tales of rape and torture I've been exposed to in twenty years. Another reported incident and the tape plays while I pale and perspire, reliving my own "incident." The tape is suppressed then until the next time the button is pushed and it rolls again. And the tape gets longer. My mind is the haunt of Richard Speck, Westeley Allan Dodd, Jeffrey Dahmer, and I didn't even allow myself to read the gory details.

The aftermath includes not being able to see movies with too much suspense, let alone violence or savagery to women, children, animals, anything helpless. Even my once beloved Edgar Allan Poe is off-limits now.

The aftermath means being battle ready. Walk with keys in clenched fist. Avoid doorways. Not too close to the curb. Be aware of hiding places: posts, poles, under cars. Never walk alone. Never lose the ability to kill.

Not long after I was raped I took karate, getting black and blue trying to ward off knife attacks and punches during practice. I spent a night applying cold compresses to my arms. Now I have a long-barreled single-shot .22 Magnum Ruger. It's less personal but more efficient than using a tiger paw to gouge out a man's eyes. I can hit the black bull's-eye at our local target range. When I can hit dead center most of the time, I'll graduate to the human figure target. And when I can accurately shoot between the eyes or right smack in the heart, I'll be very satisfied.

I think men are handsome and sexy, funny and vulnerable. Many are kind. Many are incapable of emotion. Many are trying to adapt to a world of women as equals. But those who jealously control the lives of their wives and children, I hate. They can't control life so they command their loved ones and seldom relinquish control until someone is dead. And those who stalk women and children as weak things, savoring a vision of their suffering, I fear.

One thing more. My best friend, who gave up her life to take care of me after the rape, who comforted me, gave me support and allowed me space, became my first same-sex lover. We just celebrated our nineteen-year anniversary together, and we're very happy. She tries to protect me from headlines and comforts me after nightmares. And she allows me to initiate sex. I won't be taken against my will by anyone, not even her. I will not be out of my own control.

And now that this telling is done, let the debris settle back down to the bottom and remain there, hidden by murky waters, unruffled by currents and tides, indistinguishable from the dirt.

19

The First Day of the Rest of My Life

*

At the age of twenty-seven, this woman left her husband and her small town and moved to "the city" with her two young sons. Needing to find a job, she set out immediately to buy a newspaper. As she was walking down a city street, two men grabbed her and shoved her into the backseat of their car. They both raped her and then dumped her on the side of a road.

After sending her story to me, she called to report the impact that writing down the long-term effects had on her. She explained that after she realized how difficult the previous twenty-one years had been, she decided to carry cayenne pepper spray on her key chain because she did not want to be a victim again. Soon after, she went out for a walk and a man tried to grab her purse. She sprayed him in the eyes with the cayenne pepper spray, kicked him in the groin, and ran to safety.

When I was raped, blame came into play immediately. My husband told me that it never would have happened if I had not left him. I had to agree—if I had not left him, I would not have been on that street at that time. It has taken me twenty-one years to forgive myself and to realize that I did not deserve to carry that blame.

At that time, there were no private mental hospitals. After I was found, I was put in the state hospital (for the criminally insane). They called my husband, who was cruel to me. My only other support was my mother, who told me that if I did not go back to my husband, she would make sure that I never saw my sons again.

After our sons were born, my husband wanted nothing to do with me. I tried to talk to him about life, but he would not respond. I got the feeling that he had only been interested in me as a breeder to produce sons. He could have cared less if I walked out of his life as long as he had his sons. That is why I left. But I was not willing to live without my children, so I went back. I knew that they needed him.

That is why I have stayed with my husband all of these years. That is why I drank. I am now a recovering alcoholic, but for years I used alcohol as a crutch against the pain.

Other ways in which the rape affected my life: I "need" to always sit in the front seat of a car. When I am home by myself, I turn on most of the lights and I sleep with a night-light on. I still don't sleep the whole night—I will wake up at a certain time, jump out of bed, pace back and forth. I have to look out the window and check the shadows. I will get an anxiety attack every now and then, which makes me "pig out" on junk food (my security blanket). I can get emotionally disorganized and find it difficult to make concrete decisions. I still have a few nightmares, which leave me in cold sweats. I am not comfortable wearing dresses (I will only wear one on special occasions). I have never worn low-cut or see-through blouses. I *refuse* to wear solid red or anything made of polyester (I wore this the night I was raped). I talk out loud to myself when I'm tired or fearful. I am very uncomfortable being examined by male doctors. I don't like my breasts touched or even looked at—the rapists violated them. I don't totally trust men (except my therapist). I *will not* stay in a space where all present are male. (If I'm waiting for a bus or if I'm at a meeting, I will wait for another woman to enter.)

Despite these effects, I try to lead a positive life. I have a kind and loving therapist who helps me to find my own strength and courage to love myself. I listen to healing tapes. I take walks. I take bubble baths. I greet every morning with, "This is the first day of the rest of my life." I do volunteer work with the "Buddy Program." I became a "buddy" to a person with AIDS. I meet new friends and learn so much from these truly wonderful human beings. This is so rewarding because I get so much love and so many hugs. My first "buddy" died this year. I'm preparing a panel for the AIDS quilt for him.

Recently, my husband and I learned that one of our sons has a disease. My husband broke down for the first time in his life. In his sorrow, he admitted to me that he was the one to blame for my being raped. He had been the problem, not me. Finally I was released from all of the guilt and shame. I have finally forgiven myself. I wish that he would have been able to support me and tell me sooner. It is awful how something like blame can wreak havoc. My hope now is that he will see a therapist with me.

I know that I'm coming close to the end of my healing journey because I gave back the shame to the rapists. They are guilty, not me. I would like to end my story with my favorite prayer:

SERENITY PRAYER

God grant me the serenity to
accept the things I cannot change,
the courage to change the things I can
and the wisdom to know the difference.

20

Who Cares If the Gun Was Loaded?

❨

Karen Ford LaVigne

Karen writes, "I was drinking my morning coffee and trying to read the newspaper. Trying—I have three children who seem to need me the most when I'm reading the paper. My second cup was getting cold as I turned the page to an article about a woman who was researching the long-term effects of rape. It was a very long article; I read every word. A phone number was included for those who wanted to share their stories.

"I don't remember walking to the phone or dialing. I remember not being clear during the conversation. All that was clear to me was that it was finally time to deal with having been raped. For many years, during conversations with women who had similar experiences, my standard line was, 'I was raped when I was eighteen by two guys at gunpoint.' That's all I said; that's all I felt. The rape was tucked away in some tiny little space in my head, not to be seen nor felt. Now was the time to let it out.

"For weeks I looked for safe places and times free from children and husband to allow myself to work through this shit. I cried hysterically in the bathtub, told my story to my women's meditation group, finally told my husband, and most important allowed myself to see it, feel it, and begin to heal from it. After twenty-three years, the space turned out to be not so tiny and not just in my head. The rape was in my body, my heart, my relationships, my perceptions of the world and my reactions to the world."

It was the fall of 1969 . . . following the "Summer of Love" and Woodstock. I was a go-go dancer. I lived in a downtown apartment with a fellow dancer while saving money to find my own place.

While waiting for a bus to take me to the club where my agent had booked me, a car pulled up. One of the two guys in the car said he recognized me from a nearby college bar. After chatting a few minutes, they offered me a ride to work. I felt no reservations in accepting. After all, the "Summer of Love" had been full of beautiful encounters with young people from all over the country.

A few minutes into the ride, I realized we weren't heading in the right direction. I pointed it out and was reassured all was "cool." We would get there.

After the same observation and response a second and third time, I became nervous—not afraid—that I wouldn't get to work on time. Eventually, the car pulled off the road, into a large open space, and they turned off the headlights. I was forced into the backseat and raped by the two men at gunpoint. One of them became angry with me because I would not act like I was enjoying myself.

They finished. They drove me back to town. They dropped

me off at a freeway exit near where they had picked me up. One of them said he would shoot me if I turned around to look at the license plate.

————

I made my way back to my apartment. I needed someone to help me . . . someone to tell me what to do . . . what to feel . . . how to feel.

I called my agent and explained why I wasn't at work. She said she'd call the club. I called my mother. I asked her what to do. She asked my father, who said, "How in the hell am I supposed to know what she should do?" My mother could not offer advice. My agent called back. She said the club owner was angry—he couldn't understand why I couldn't come to dance at his club. Couldn't I just shower? He wouldn't be mad if I was late! I didn't go to dance at his club. I did shower.

I called the police. They eventually showed up, put me in the backseat of a car, and grilled me. I remember some of the questions: "Do you wear a bra?" "Are you pregnant and making up this story so your parents won't get mad?" "How do you know the gun was loaded?"

Eventually I ended up in some emergency room, where I was examined, questioned further, and passed back and forth between medical and police interrogators. I don't remember much of the rest of the night. Some days later I went to police headquarters to look at mug shot books. I couldn't find pictures of the rapists. The police asked me to drop charges. I wouldn't.

Some weeks later at the free VD clinic, I waited for hours with dozens of other women. My guess is that I was the only one who was not a prostitute. A young male medical resident examined me and tested me for venereal diseases. When he was finished, he became belligerent. He said that he was disgusted with me and that I was an unworthy human being. He left the room when I started to cry. A round, ample-bosomed nurse came in and held me. She stroked my hair, my face, and my back. I felt safe. As I calmed down, she asked me why I was crying. I told her what the doctor had said. She sat me in a chair, walked out briskly, and returned with him. She then told him I was a victim of rape. She told him that if he was to be a successful doctor he needed to show care and compassion and never to jump to conclusions. She would not allow him to treat me with disrespect. She then demanded he apologize. He did.

The rapists weren't caught. Most of my life continued.

The biggest effect for me was the loss of feeling safe with my sexuality. But did I ever feel safe before the rape? I remember dozens of incidents in my life to the contrary: being fondled by old men, ogled by men in cars as I walked down the street (even in grade school) who asked, "Hey, baby, wanna ride?," groped by boys on the playground as they ran by, told by society that "boys will be boys," disregarded by my father if I didn't meet some unspoken standard he had set for me.

Feeling safe . . . I don't ever remember feeling safe, except with that nurse.

I blame my abnormal sexual response on being raped. I'm married. My husband is caring, patient, nonthreatening. We have a relationship built on trust, growth as individuals and as a couple, support, love, understanding. However, when we're in bed I tense. My entire body coils for action, ready to push away my attacker. In the twelve years we have been together, I remember very few times when I didn't think of being raped while making love. I remember the rapists, the doctor, the police officers, my parents, and the question "How did you know the gun was loaded?"

I have felt trapped, as if I were a continued prisoner of the rape. Freedom is now slowly approaching. With the help of friends, body workers, a mind-body connection therapist, thera-peutic touch, and prayer, I'm learning strength through allowing myself to be vulnerable sometimes. To be vulnerable does not mean Karen, the woman, has to be a victim. I'm finding strength in the feminine.

My body is also healing. I've had many physical ailments on the left side of my body—hip, shoulder, and neck. Through therapeutic touch and movement and body therapies, these ailments are being resolved. I remember that I was restrained by one rapist holding me down by my left shoulder. This came back to me during some body work for muscle spasms and bursitis in my left shoulder, which has now been resolved. Similar memories followed during sessions to heal my left hip and pelvis. Sex was always painful in my left hip. It was inflexible. When I did move my hip normally, tendons would snap across the bone—more painful, horrible memories trapped in my left hip. Many therapy sessions later, normal movement is returning. Movement is freer. Running, dancing, playing, and sex are joyfully spontaneous. My mind and heart are also returning to joy.

It's a long, slow painful road. There is beautiful warm light at the end of the tunnel. Maybe someday I can get to the forgiveness stage. At this point I have no forgiveness for my rapists, only contempt and hatred. At times I really deeply hope they have been hurt as much as I have. I believe that by being a victim, only then can one realize how dreadfully wrong it is to get joy and pleasure from another's agony.

Rape is a symptom of our society's male-dominated, female-oppressive views. When love and respect for women and women's bodies are absent, how then can we live in harmony with all life? How can we have respect for life?

Oh yes . . . something positive came from this experience. I am a registered nurse. I *never* let anyone treat one of my patients with disrespect. I make sure that I always do the best job I can to ensure my patients aren't victimized by the health care system. I make sure they feel safe in my care.

21

From Milk House to No House

❨

This woman writes, "When I read the article in the newspaper requesting input on the long-term effects of rape, my first response was 'if only this could really be known.' I got mad, actually felt sick, and my mind began racing through my past—one I have to dismiss off and on. But, oh, it has always resurfaced and it always will. I felt my involvement in this study could possibly help release a part of the anger, hurt, and bitterness I have carried and lived with for years. I'm nearly thirty-seven years old. I've dealt with the first rape since I was thirteen, and I have experienced eight rapes. Yes, eight. Why so many times you may ask? Didn't I learn not to be in a situation where it may happen again? Am I that stupid? It's taken me years to realize the true answers to these questions."

THIRTEEN YEARS OLD—My dad was out in the field bailing hay. My mother went to town for supplies. I was unloading the hay wagon with a neighbor man who was helping my father. We unloaded the last bail into the haymow and walked to the milk house for some cool water from the water hose, a common practice during the summer. At first I thought this guy was joking around. We knew him well—he, his wife, and his kids were always welcome at our house and we frequented their house also.

———————

Having my clothes removed was so embarrassing, but I couldn't help it. What was he hurting me for? I was pinned up against the milk tank by his strength. Sex! Sex is dirty! My mom told me so! I'm crying—I'm bleeding—I'm scared. My feet haven't touched the ground for so long. Please stop . . . please . . . you're hurting me. Put me down! No! Please don't choke me anymore! I'll behave! Why are you hugging me and smiling? Did I do something good? No, I promise I won't tell anybody—ever. No, please don't tell my mom I was bad. You know Dad will beat me again! I do love my kitty—I don't want her to die . . .

———————

But, you know, at age thirteen I came to realize, "Maybe this is what it takes to be liked. Maybe this is why my mom and dad never kiss me, hug me, or tell me they love me. I wish Dad would hug me instead." Oh, WHY did this happen to me? I'm so confused. I'm alone.

I grew up on a dairy farm in Wisconsin with eight brothers and sisters. My childhood was cold and lonely. It was well known throughout the family and neighborhood that I was the "black sheep" of the family. If something went wrong or someone did something wrong, I was used as the example. Discipline, as long as I can remember, was very abusive, filled with massive, sometimes bleeding, welts and bruises and bizarre and cruel punishments. This was common treatment from my parents as well as five of my brothers and sisters until I ran away.

I hated school because I never had time to do the homework, resulting in ridicule and embarrassment for me. I had no friends to talk to because I was shy and my clothes smelled like a barn. I missed having a childhood because of work that had to be done on the farm. I never experienced the prom, school events, dating, or graduation. I watched everyone around me receive class rings, yearbooks, and senior pictures. Me, I ran away halfway through my senior year. I was seventeen years old.

If I got really desperate or really lonely, sex was the answer. I was loved for an evening or two and then I'd go on with my life. I learned what men were all about early and had a very low opinion of them. Use them before they use you was an attitude I was learning to accept. I began to hate men for what they stood for—sex, strength, abuse, cruelty.

EIGHTEEN YEARS OLD, NAMPA, IDAHO—My second rape occurred in Idaho. An acquaintance along with four of his buddies came to pick me up after work, asking if I wanted to go to a big party. I said "sure" and got into the car with my "friend."

Little did I know that I was to be "the party"—beaten, gagged, tied up, and sexually used in every way possibly imaginable for seven days and eight nights. I lived in horror and overheard them say that I would not get out of this alive, as I could identify them. If their perverted requests were not met upon command, I was beaten with a wet leather belt that was soaking in a pail of water. They demanded that my first and only response to each command be a military style "Sir-Yes-Sir!" When they left for work in the mornings, my hands, legs, and mouth were bound for the day. I was, however, untied each night to cook their dinner and allowed one hour to clean their apartment.

The eighth evening, they were done with me, talked about their next unsuspecting victim, and decided it was time to dispose of me. Four of them took their last thrills with me, and then I was tied up into a small lump and stuffed into a military duffel bag. My final destination—the Nampa River. To this day, I have no idea who saved me or how I was saved. I do, however, remember dying . . .

My recovery was long. My mental bruises will never go away. On the outside, I still looked OK. I survived. I was only eighteen and had a full life ahead of me.

NINETEEN YEARS OLD, CALDWELL, IDAHO—My boss invited me for dinner at his parents' house after a fine, relaxing afternoon of motorcycle riding. I really liked this guy and had dated him for about a month without having sex. After dinner we went for a ride in his car with his daughter before he'd be dropping her off at home.

Before I realized that we were out in the boonies somewhere, he stopped the car and raped me as his four-year-old daughter watched. For fighting him off and continually saying "no" I was repeatedly slugged in the face and stomach with his fist until I gave in.

I never saw him again, never went back to work. I just packed up and left the state.

TWENTY-ONE YEARS OLD, COLORADO SPRINGS, COLORADO—I found my first true love here. Approximately a year into our common-law marriage, my fourth rape took place. We decided we needed some chips and soda. My husband offered to go, but I said that I would go, since he was already comfortable for the evening. It was dark, but it was a trip I had often made, no more than a block across the street from our apartment complex.

The car slowed down behind me. I heard it and turned around to look, ready to run if it was someone who was going to harass me. It seemed I was always on guard.

"Lookin' fine, lady. How about a ride?"

"No thanks. My husband's waiting for me," I stated firmly as I kept walking. The car went ahead of me and the doors opened. The guns were pointed at me and I froze.

"Get in, bitch," he said softly. "You make a scene and you are dead."

Do I call his bluff? I'm scared. Should I scream? No. They look crazy enough to shoot. As I slowly walked to the car and got into the backseat as instructed, I thought, NO. Why me, Lord? I felt weak; my stomach was turning.

As they drove up into the mountains, my mind raced. Cooperate and you won't get hurt. I cooperated. They took their turns with me. I kept my eyes closed and it was over. No beatings—only threats. I promised I would not turn them in. They didn't hurt me physically. I asked them to please just take me back to the 7-Eleven. To my disbelief, that's exactly what they did.

The police report was filed and the routine tests were done. The questions, though, were totally humiliating. I was not treated as the victim. They asked me questions like: What were you wearing? Did you provoke them? Did you have an orgasm? Why didn't you run instead? Were you turned on by either of these two men at any point in time? Can you describe each of their penises? Describe the penetration in detail. These were all being asked by a male officer. Where was the "I know this must be hard on you. Here's a tissue" or "We need to ask you some very embarrassing questions. Are you up to answering them?"

The following day, one of the two rapists was brought in for questioning but was let go on technicalities. Why? There were no bruises. The car I described was blue with rust, not dark green with rust, and the tape case I described in the backseat was no longer there. The rapist said that he had never seen me before.

My husband was no support after the initial shock. We stayed together though and tried to forget—until I became pregnant. I was given a choice of him or the kid. I chose my child. My son is nearly seventeen years old now, and it is a choice I have never regretted.

TWENTY-THREE YEARS OLD, MASSACHUSETTS—A year after our divorce, I was brutally raped by my ex-husband.

———

I was chased down, followed everywhere, harassed at my work place, and traumatized continually. Approximately eleven one evening, I woke up to the sounds of cursing, threats, and my door being kicked in. He was drunk. I tried to escape several times. Before this ordeal was over, I was beaten, raped, stabbed deeply in my upper arm, and cut deeply between the legs. He left me lying on the floor that early morning with the words, "Now I won't have to worry about you with other men!" You see, he had always threatened, "If I can't have you, neither will anyone else." He left me to die, to bleed to death. I was weak. I had no control over my movements. I tried to crawl to the phone for help. I couldn't. I think I passed out. When I woke up I was in the hospital with tubes and needles everywhere. How I made it through this—again—I'll never know.

———

I've always thought someone was looking over me, but if that was true, why did I have to go through all of this in the first place? At age twenty-three, I was still a survivor. I was even more confused than before, but . . . life goes on and so did I. My dating stopped. My son was my life when I wasn't working.

On the one hand I hated men and anything they stood for. On the other hand, I craved to be loved and held. I always dreamed of the perfect family—one boy, one girl, a loving husband, and me. I was very cautious regarding abusive behavior and knew I was beyond this.

I remarried in 1981. I thought this marriage would last the rest of my life. But instead of physical abuse, I was mentally and emotionally abused. I was no longer an individual. I was a mold. For seven years my moves consisted of whatever he and his mother wanted them to be. I was like a puppet on a string. I remember wondering which was worse: physical or mental abuse. At least you could heal on the outside.

My husband's family was well known, and they were considered to be upstanding citizens. They were business owners, and their other son was a police officer. Financially we were secure, and we had a beautiful three-thousand-square-foot home. I was determined to make this work. I could not be a failure again. My father even loved me by now, and when I'd visit back home, I'd hear how I turned out to be a favorite. People thought my husband and I were very compatible. My son liked him.

Sex was a big problem for me throughout our marriage, but he always made it known that it was one of the best things we had going. I had already learned to fake it well. I loved him, so it didn't matter to me. I'd handle it. I did what he liked and I never told him how disgusting he was to me sexually. He knew of my past and assured me he'd work with me on it but never did. Talking to him went in one ear and out the other. It was nothing to him to do it twice a day, and as time went on it seemed his sexual urge got stronger. If I tried to talk and slow him down he'd be insulted and think I didn't love him. So instead I lived in misery and guilt and gave in to him. My attitude became, "Hurry and get it over with, you big pig." I begged for counseling, but his family did not believe in it, so that was hopeless.

After seven years of marriage I couldn't handle it anymore. I was suffocating. I began to stand up to my in-laws and stand up for my rights. I became an obsessed workaholic. I would also avoid cuddling (something I actually enjoyed), as I knew it always led to sex. I'd pray he'd fall asleep on the couch watching TV so that I'd be safe for the night. I resented my life. I knew I deserved better.

After ten years of marriage, I was single again. It was a devastating feeling. I was scared. I was a failure—again. Between him and his mother, they made sure I was left with nothing. *They made sure I was nothing.* But life was supposed to go on and I still had a beautiful seven-year-old daughter and fourteen-year-old son to fight for.

THIRTY-FOUR YEARS OLD—My new landlord, the owner of the house I rented two weeks after the separation, took advantage of a mentally and physically exhausted individual. He was a family practice physician, a prominent doctor. We talked some. He invited me to go to dinner at a local restaurant. I declined. I just wanted to shower and go to sleep after such an active day of moving. He left. I remember thinking as my head hit the pillow what a gross-looking guy he was, that I would never go to a doctor who looked like him—fat, big, ugly. He reminded me of one of those sumo wrestlers.

I was awakened by the doctor about three hours later. He said I was having a nightmare and that he was just trying to comfort me. I thanked him and told him I was OK, that I just wanted to be alone. He wanted to talk. I didn't. He had one thing in mind.

He started touching me. I got mad! I tried to stay calm. I begged him to leave. I cried, "I don't need this. Please just leave me alone. You're a doctor. Doctors don't do this." He didn't need to use so much strength on me. I had none. As he pinned me down, he removed my oversize T-shirt and panties as he kept repeating, "You need this. It'll calm your nerves. You need this. I'll help you." He stood up to remove his clothing, and I tried to cover up. I was too emotionally and physically spent even to try to get away. I just lay there crying. Is this what it's all about? Is this what I have to look forward to? I lay there. I was lifeless. He did his manly thing. I didn't fight. I made it to the bathroom. I threw up. I showered. I cried. I locked myself in the bathroom for the rest of the night.

———————

I did not turn him into the police. I feared my soon-to-be ex-husband would find out from his cop brother. A week later he used his key to get in and forced his way again. What did I do? Nothing! I was powerless. I was lost. I couldn't bring myself any more shame. I couldn't handle another court case, dragging myself through this all over again. Suicide was on my mind constantly. I was in acute depression. But I had two beautiful children. They kept me going! Of course I couldn't tell them what was going on, but I had to stay strong for them.

There are two rapes I cannot write about. I live with them inside.

Initially, therapy did not help much. I was put on Prozac—it didn't solve my problems. May 9, 1992. I couldn't handle it anymore. I gave up. I tried to commit suicide. I ended up alive and in the hospital. I cried, "Why!" I even failed at this. I had sent suicide letters out hours before, but I'm still here. How embarrassing . . .

I'm two months shy of turning thirty-seven years old. I go on with my life, but I need a new one. I'm afraid to be alone yet scared to have a relationship. I refuse to be hurt again, so I deprive myself of any chance for a relationship. I've been divorced now for a year and a half. I've lost all security—a home, my husband, my business, and custody of my two children to my ex-husband as of January 1992.

The therapist I see now tells me I've got to learn to show my anger, that I have poor judgment skills, that it's OK to be mad, that I need to put the past behind me, that I don't need to be a walking time bomb. I have no problem now saying, "One day I will make it. The past can be put behind me." But for now, I'm bitter and I'm hurt. I know I am a good person. I'm a very likable person. I'm attractive and I know that if I wanted to, I could pick or choose a number of men. But I also know that until my life gets straightened out, this would not be fair to myself or to anyone else.

I have a long road ahead of me. I can do it. I have to do it. Through therapy I can see patterns I have followed. I can see areas of improvement. I can see why I was so vulnerable. I often wondered if there was a sign written across my forehead, "Pick me! I can easily be raped!" Or was it that I just had an aura about me, "I'm vulnerable—you'll get away with it."

Incidentally, I must add a note about a bit of pleasure that I have experienced in this lifetime nightmare. At age thirty-five, I finally had a real orgasm. I finally experienced sexual pleasure— total satisfaction. I didn't have to fake it. This was natural, a new experience for me. Now that's progress!

22

From American Citizen to Government Property

❮

PTSD, or is it TPDS
Whatever . . . I have it

It sounds like
a sexually transmitted disease

Or is it some kind of fluid
to fix my car?

Post Traumatic Stress Disorder
What a catchy title for

Girl, your brain is all f——d up!

Kathleen was an enlisted junior petty officer in the U.S. Navy. She was raped by a senior petty officer twenty-four years ago, ten days short of her twenty-first birthday.

The navy was going to be a new start for me. Having been raised in a very large Roman Catholic family by a mother who was mentally ill, I had never been allowed to be a child, much less a teenage girl. I entered the navy on my twentieth birthday, ready to finally experience independence.

Only the very best women were allowed into the navy during the Vietnam years. Not only did we have to have a high school diploma, we also had to have been in the top thirty percent of our class. At the same time, men did not even have to have a diploma. Our lives were checked over with magnifying glasses. We were the very best from the most traditional American families. We were intelligent and sensitive and caring and dedicated people, but ignorant of worldly ways.

I entered an environment that was incredibly hostile toward me based solely upon my gender. There were never more than four or five women in a school of three thousand. We were forced to walk gauntlets. While physical contact did not occur each time, verbal abuse and threats were incessant. The problem with verbal abuse is that it leaves no apparent scars. It was very easy not to see the scars myself, and so certainly nobody else saw them. But it is the soul that does not forget any abuse.

After I was raped, this atmosphere created much confusion for me. In uniform I was considered "one of the best." I had admirals vying for my talents through the Pentagon. I received special assignments, awards, and commendations. Out of uniform I was considered nothing but a physical object that was forced to endure what men saw fit for their own purposes.

My immediate response to the rape was to believe that it had occurred because I was attractive. So I decided to become unattractive. I let my hair grow scraggly, I stopped wearing makeup and I deliberately overate.

I am very susceptible to stress because I have had so very much in my life. The way I have always dealt with it is to internalize it. Thirteen months after the rape, I had a massive intestinal hemorrhage.

Because I was a woman, the military doctors initially insisted that I had attempted an abortion on myself. Then they accused me of taking drugs. I had a top secret clearance, so the doctors would not treat me until they got a new background check from the FBI and naval intelligence. Eighteen days passed before they even did a GI series. Of course, they found nothing by that time.

They believed that I had taken some kind of drug that had eaten a hole in my stomach and that the tissue had healed before they had had a chance to find it. I was even accused of deliberately eating ground glass. I was so incensed that when one of the medical students asked me about it, I answered sarcastically, "Oh yes, I sprinkled it on my breakfast each morning." The doctor in charge told me that he and his fellow commissioned officers would not tolerate insubordination from an enlisted woman. They even talked about using me to experiment with exploratory surgery.

After my discharge from the hospital, I still experienced problems that the hospital doctors could not diagnose. They were angry with me because my command doctor wanted them to perform more tests until a diagnosis could be made. At that point, I was sodomized by one of the hospital doctors and told never to return to the hospital. I reported this to my command doctor who apologized for sending me there.

I received an honorable discharge with a ten percent disability for my medical condition. Even though I had reported the rape, the navy did not consider it in calculating the amount of disability I was due. At that time, I just wanted out. As a civilian I found that either my "self" or my space was still being accosted. I was incredibly threatened if someone insisted on making eye contact with me. I avoided blond, thin, mousy-looking men because those were the physical characteristics of the rapist. I did not like going places where I knew I would meet people. I became more and more antisocial. My fears increased to the point that even years later I still did not go anywhere without my husband or children.

This lasted until my husband died in 1987. With my knight in shining armor gone, I had to find the strength to get me through. At first I took my children with me everywhere. Then I decided that I really had to start going places alone.

Throughout these years, I had continued to overeat, and, after each child, I gained large amounts of weight. I tried to lose it, but I became fearful as soon as friends noticed. I figured that if they noticed, then the rest of the world did too. I inevitably put it back on. I followed this pattern until my husband died. His death was once again a catalyst for change. I lost ninety pounds. All of a sudden, I had men who were stumbling over each other to open doors for me. This made me angry because these men would not have done this for me ninety pounds ago! I did not feel comfortable at that weight because I was afraid that my defenses were gone, so I put a few pounds back on. I still had to go through some grieving time for the loss of the fat woman who had protected me all of those years. I don't think that I will ever go back to that weight, but it is still something that I miss—the feeling that I was safe.

I have hoped that eventually I will be able to feel secure and not always be vigilant about how many men are near me. It has been difficult for me to be in government buildings because I was raped in one. I was locked in and could not get out. If I were to be attacked in an open space, I feel that at least I could fight and run. As soon as I walk into a government building, my antennae go up. I immediately start counting men and noting where they are, what they are doing and if they are watching me.

Because of the medical abuse in the navy, I have a very difficult time trusting doctors. I will not allow a rectal exam. I decided years ago that I would rather bleed to death or die of cancer than undergo that type of exam. I know that I should get a pap smear every year, but I don't. I even have a difficult time trusting women doctors. I can sit and talk to them forever. But when it comes time for a physical exam, I feel really desperate. For my precancerous intestinal condition, I have to undergo biopsies periodically. My greatest fear is that they will find something such that I will need surgery. I have an incredible dread of surgery because I have a terrible fear of loss of control.

I have practically no faith in organized religions because the Catholic priests in the navy were so terrible to me. They had told me that women in the navy were there to service men sexually and that I was incredibly ignorant for not knowing that. Now that I knew it, if I did not stop making a big deal out of it, I would not marry and produce sons for the church. I have not been a practicing Catholic since just after I was raped. Throughout the years, I have mentioned these statements to a number of priests who have invariably called me a liar. I did find one bishop who agreed that it probably happened, but he nonetheless blamed me for my expectation of receiving help with the issue of rape. "Priests are not trained to counsel. They are strictly for spiritual guidance," he stated.

Authority figures have been a problem for me because they had abused me and had denied that it had ever happened. My suppressed anger began manifesting itself in my dreams. I was grinding my teeth together so hard that the pain of it was waking me up. My psychiatrist instructed me on how to wake myself up during dreams. I had not consciously known that I was that angry. Then, in talking with my psychiatrist, I realized that I was afraid of expressing the anger because I was not sure what I would do with it. We worked on this, and now I no longer wake up at night clenching my teeth.

Until just a few years ago, I had neither the time nor the

energy to address these problems. My husband, a Vietnam combat veteran, died after battling Agent Orange–related cancers for years. His illness had superceded all things. I had made the choice to subjugate all of my personal needs and desires in order to facilitate his comfort and security. Only when he died was I able to deal with my problems without any sense of guilt. It's been an eye opener for me to have time to think about what I would like to do.

Until three years ago, I would have contended that the rape had not affected my sexuality. I had a good relationship with my husband, but he was very ill for many years. He was a considerate man and very sexually knowledgeable, but I did not seem to be behaving the way he thought I should. My body was not reacting to him the way he thought it should. I thought I was doing just fine. I had had relations with a few men before my husband came along, and it was the same thing. They didn't complain that I wasn't good in bed; they just felt that they weren't doing something right because I wasn't satisfied. They would get very angry with me. My husband just seemed to understand, and after a while he quit saying anything about it.

Then I met my current fiancé. At the age of forty-three, I finally discovered what had been missing all of my life—a true sense of trust. It is such a wonderful feeling. It is not just that the sex is great, but I really have a close, safe feeling. I wasn't really sure that I would ever have a relationship with a man who was not afraid to tell me that he loved me, was not afraid to let me know that he appreciated me, had trust that I would be there for him. It is such a wholesome, healing type of love, and he is so understanding of my peculiarities.

He has seen a great deal of tragedy in his twenty-four years of law enforcement and knows how to be with a person who has experienced violence. My husband would get so frustrated. He wanted me to tell him how to make it all better; I told him he couldn't. He wanted to fix it. If he couldn't, he felt that it was his fault. My fiancé does not feel that way. He listens and truly understands. That's all that I need—someone who understands, someone who doesn't criticize or judge or give suggestions on how I should really be doing better. This helps me to be open and understanding for him as well.

When word of the Tailhook Scandal broke, I received a phone call from an Associated Press reporter. She stated that she was aware that I had been raped while serving in the navy and asked if I would consider telling my story. She could not tell me how she knew, but I suspect that someone familiar with my file had shown it to her.

For over twenty years, I never thought about doing anything because I knew that I had to help myself before I could help others. Now my daughter and her friends are at the age when some of them are actually considering the military, and I ask myself, "What have I done?" I have tried so hard to make this world a better place for my children, but I have done nothing in respect to the military. I do not want my daughters to go through what I did.

After my story broke, a congresswoman said that she had been receiving hundreds of letters not only from women veterans and women still in the military but also an equal number from fathers and husbands of women who were too afraid or unable to come forward. Following this, I wrote letters to my congressional delegation and to senior members of the Veteran Affairs Committee and the Armed Forces Committee detailing the rape as well as the unacceptable treatment I received following it. I received a letter back from one of the senators stating that my letter would be put into the Congressional Record. He wanted me to know that my experiences would not go unresolved or be forgotten, that the wrongs that have been committed against women would be righted no matter the cost. I find that difficult to believe because there is no branch of the navy that is not pathologically hostile toward women. The entire system is involved. It is going to take a lot more than just not promoting somebody, because the military actually condones sexual harassment.

I don't feel guilty that I did not do something before because I was not ready. I am now. My daughter said to me, "Mom, you are so courageous!" I think the people who are courageous are the young women who are still in the military or who just got out and are coming forward. They are the ones who really have courage. I have had all of these years to learn how to cope and deal. They are just beginning. I don't really think of it as being courageous. I just feel that it is time, that it needed to be done and I did it.

23

Frightened Fighter

❨

Your age at the time of the rape(s)
6, 9, 11, 17, 22
Your present age 31
You are female X   male .
The rapist(s) was known 3
unknown 4 to you.
If known, indicate relationship
stepfather, father, boyfriends, husband, strangers
(Optional) Did you report the
rape to law officials? No X Yes X

FRIGHTENED FIGHTER

Remembering makes my heart race
My blood runs wild and hot
Their hands, their breath, their words
become adrenaline

Lies are lies
Murder is murder
Rape is an excuse
Excuses for everything

Anger is too small of a word
Men are a different species
Excuses for everything
They never want to fix the damage

Your rage is no excuse to make me suffer
Am I just as bad as you are now
I get meaner and colder as time goes by
I will never take that walk again

My want is not clear
Why, when, and where make no sense
Crying doesn't take it away
Nightmares become a dream of revenge

Physically or mentally
I'm heavier than I've ever been
I don't want someone to like me
For my body or for my mind.

Your word against theirs
No proof
Fight it
Each day I fight with myself

24

Out of Darkness

)

Michele writes, "Rape creates something in all of us—the severe trauma of loss. This loss shows itself in many areas of our emotional selves, from the extremes of oblivion to the most perfect facades of seemingly functioning personae. Often accompanying loss is shame and guilt. Rape survivors have been told that if we were in a situation in which we were raped, it was somehow our fault. This belief can be changed by starting with ourselves. We cannot do the recovery process alone. We need others' assistance and love and representation of healing. We need to see that it is possible and probable.

I wrote the following poem as a reflection of what has transpired over my decades of healing."

I have come over the mountain range of desperation
and traveled through the ocean bellies of mournful emotions.
Across the black abyss of turmoil,
I climbed the steep cliffs of struggle to face myself.
In faith I rose to the Brilliance
I entered the doorway of light and tasted freedom,
I found my Self and God within.

I was raped when I was barely an adult, but abuse was not foreign to me. I was abused and sexually violated throughout my
childhood. So the long-term effects of the rape were com-
pounded and colored by the effects of years of abuse and by the
convolutions of my self-perception. When someone is raped, the
tendency is to blame oneself. What have I done to deserve this?
is the resounding question. There is no answer.

I had a strong but secret love for God, so my questions were: Is
God punishing me? Why does God want to punish me? If God is
a loving God, why would I live a life of maltreatment? Something
must be wrong and why do I always feel it's with me? The self-
blame was overwhelming.

In 1968, I met the man who raped me through a friend who
was concerned with his welfare. We went to his apartment. He
was hungry and broke, so he said. Being nineteen, compassionate, and rescuing, the following week I went through my home
freezer and packed two bags of food. When I brought them to
him, I also offered some cash, which he took. He started acting
odd—his words were suggestive and crude. I did not know what
was happening.

———

I vaguely remember an invitation of sex. I grabbed my purse to
leave and he grabbed me. I was only five four and he was over six
feet. He dragged me into his bedroom. I was fighting him with

punches, kicks, and screams. I continually screamed NO! I hit his face and tried to kick his genital area but was unsuccessful. Then I tried to plead with him to let me go. He ripped my clothes off, pinned my arms down with one hand, unzipped his pants and forcefully penetrated my vagina. I recollect shrieking in pain and hoping someone would hear me. This idea was futile.

I remember crying afterward as I sat on the bedroom floor in total shock at what had just occurred. Guilty thoughts were engulfing my mind: "I am in a man's apartment. I am married and my husband is in Vietnam. My father is the damn base commander. I was the tramp that invited this somehow." The guilt and blame had paralyzed me.

I became aware of someone screaming. It was him yelling at me with vile words. He was throwing my purse back on the table. I froze at the screaming. This is something that was constant in my parents' house, and it paralyzed me. I picked up my purse and looked through my wallet. The bastard stole what little money was left. I was angry at the theft. The physical violation had not made its impact. I asked for it back. He started to swing at me. I wanted out! I ran for the sliding glass doors and ran to my car. He was behind me; I was quicker. I pulled my car out of the driveway. This was the last time I saw him, but later I did hear he had raped several more women.

———

I took the guilt of the rape and made it my responsibility. Why do I deserve this continuous violent abuse? What have I done bad or wrong? Why do I deserve this? How am I supposed to be? I did what I had done my entire life—I handled it myself by repressing my feelings.

I had to survive. I was staying with my parents, my mother still the violent abuser. And of course, I believed that I definitely deserved the maltreatment. It would be years before I could start to sift through this terror and denial. I did not know that my mother was abusive. I thought that I was an awful person and this was somehow normal. I was only aware that I was unhappy and did not want to live in their home anymore. I soon left their house for the second time and only visited them once more before they died many years later.

My father never gave any indication that something was wrong in our family, and he was a wing commander, base commander, and diplomat. If anyone would know, he would. I trusted him. Mom continually told me that I was bad, so I believed her. The armed services are abusive in their hierarchy and lack of regard for the family unit. An officer's position is image and image alone. This is what I grew up with, and at the time it was all I knew or could see. I was a nineteen-year-old kid who knew nothing of being on my own, or about life, much less about being trapped in a man's apartment when trying to do something nice. Later, and much later, I began to feel the anguish of my deep anger.

Dealing with all this was a long process. It took many years before I mentioned the abuse in therapy, and therapy did not come until I attempted suicide at age twenty-three. I was serious about dying. I did not want to live anymore. A friend found me at home, and thought I was dead. He called the ambulance and they took me to the hospital. The only recollection I have is of some words from a doctor in the hospital, "Don't you dare leave, you come back here." He was screaming at me, and then there was darkness. I was unconscious at that point until waking up in the intensive care unit. My rage reared its head, and I obviously resented the help I was being given.

I was committed to the psychiatric hospital because I was a danger to myself. All I wanted to do was kill myself. I had been beaten, kicked, raped, and screamed at all of my life. Why were strangers concerned if I lived. I'm a bad person. Don't these people see that? This was a rotten place to live, and if I died I knew I would leave the world a better place.

The abuse and the rape never came up in therapy at the hospital. I was told by the doctors that I was very sick and that I needed lots of help. These statements triggered all of the shame in me. Unfortunately the issue of shame was not a therapeutic process as of yet. This was twenty-two years ago. I am now forty-five.

Long-term therapy followed. First the encounter groups—discussion about shame and abusiveness. It was apparent that I had a great deal of anger (rage, to be honest), so the therapist wanted me to act it out. This was way too early for me. I was running from the violence and screaming. I did not want to act out more violence. I was told to throw a chair across the room. Although I was that angry, I could not bring myself to do such an act of violence at that moment. I wanted out of the violence! I wanted one person to talk and cry with, not a whole staff and ten group members who didn't understand my secret shames of abuse. I needed to work up to revealing the secret of how bad a person I was.

The doctors suggested I be medicated. I flatly refused. If I was going to go through this process, I was going to do it consciously. I was tired of masking and repressing. I had a highly aware, acutely active brain. I saw other patients medicated on Thorazine. "No way, José." I was going to be a functional person in my dysfunction.

The doctors were male. I continually requested women doctors, but another male doctor was recommended for outpatient therapy. I had a great amount of resistance to this. I felt trapped by a system that said I had no choice. I felt that I could not share my dark secrets with another male stranger.

I left the hospital but still was in therapy. I began college and decided to major in psychology. This subject had been of interest to me for many years. In high school I read child psychology books, searching for information about abuse. I also read law books about children's rights. Because I was adopted, I wanted to know if any loopholes existed that would allow me to separate from my parents.

The new male doctor offered a screaming room and later a small group. The screaming room was intimidating. It had two unmade beds, very little light, and I was to kick, hit, and scream therein. I tried. I could not tell him my shame and what was inside. He may have had a doctorate degree, but he was a man near a bed, and this is all I was aware of.

In his group, I was called the "whiny" one. My perception was that people did not like me. But there was a gradual breakthrough. At twenty-four, I met some simple people who would meditate on Wednesday nights. This is where I began my true spiritual growth, which spilled over into my therapy.

My therapy had taken an exciting turn—the doctor had a female intern working with him. This was a great relief. I started to open up and act out. My true nature was coming through. And the therapy group was noticing a profound change in me. One man actually said he was beginning to like me, or maybe, tolerate me. But something was changing!

The spiritual dimension was accelerating my growth. In meditation groups, I was discovering that I had a guide, and this helped to ease the deep fear that I was living alone. I could ask questions during the meditation groups to understand more about myself and why I was in this incredible quandary of horrid emotion and constant suicidal intentions. Hope lingered with each group. I started looking to gurus and swamis. I went to Eastern philosophy retreats. I studied reincarnation, Zen Buddhism, Hinduism, and the Bhagavad Gita. This gave me a sense of what was beyond the quagmire of abuse and that I did not deserve what happened to me.

But then ambivalence set in. I came to another level of the dark abyss and became aware of my intense shame. I was still committed to my search for truth but carried the haunting modes of being a victim and the desire to die with me. I wanted change in my life without leaving my spiritual life and growth.

The walls of my life were crumbling. That is when a new therapist walked into my life. This therapist helped me to stop glorifying my parents and acknowledge that my father was weak and my mother was sick and abusive. My father was the commander of thousands on an air force base, but he could not come to terms with his home life, where he had no control. He lived in denial and this I could finally see. His denial was supported by the society he lived in and the value of image over humanity. I worked with this therapist for four years, and it was beneficial work. But I still needed more. Somehow, I needed something that psychology alone could not offer: spiritual understanding.

I decided to catapult myself into a dimension of faith. And so, by whatever coincidence we can blame circumstances on, I was injured in a car accident and could not do much physically. Thereby I was given time to do the mental work that was needed.

I began reading more books and attending workshops. I kept a constant vigil of listening to tapes of many different teachers from all areas. I had an insatiable appetite. Every moment of my life was about healing and understanding myself. It was agony and ecstasy for almost two years.

The agony slowly diminished and there came an untold peace. The peace would come and then a deeper level within me would emerge. When I came back to the mainstream of life I was totally changed—no longer afraid of pain, I was eager to live. I am no longer a victim. I do not feel that God/Goddess is punishing me. I am alive and I know peace.

A couple of years ago, I wrote an article and I used the words, "I suffer with joy." In realizing that pain is natural, I feel an incredible release from the depths of my soul. I can enjoy my tears. I can let my emotions show and experience life without fear. Pain is just as natural as joy and exuberance. When we cut off the so called negative feelings, we are cutting off a vital part of ourselves. We need these pieces to be whole.

The amount of energy and commitment needed to change from the victim to the victorious is enormous. But the unshakable foundation of freedom and inner peace is the gift received in that shift. I cannot say that I have consciously reached my soul, but I truly know the "self" that is called Michele.

When I tell others that I have recovered from the trauma, they usually have one of two reactions—denial that recovery is possible, or thinking that I live in a constant state of "bliss." This is not true. I waffle in and out of love, peace, and self-doubt. Life continues to be very challenging—some days a roller coaster. I choose to live in response instead of reaction. There is no perfect way! Life is a Journey, not a destination.

The journey of healing continues. I cannot stress this point enough. Life, as in nature, is ever growing and changing, and so are our relationships to others and ourselves and our Higher Power. All the avenues that I have experienced and that will come in the future have only given me greater depth and richness in my life. God/Goddess is infinite, eternal, so it would only be wise to live and experience as many passageways as possible. The greatest secret I have discovered is that all the wisdom that anyone may seek already lives within ourselves. It only takes desire to find it.

25

And Darkness Surrounds Me

☾

I live half my life as if it never
  existed
Half my past is enshrouded in
  secrets
Shielding what others may disdain
Hiding this past in blame and
  shame
I'm a rape victim
Now darkness surrounds me

I loved to sing, I had a voice
Yet I sing others' songs with my
  feeling
My voice was taken; I had no
  choice
Will I ever sing my song with my
  voice?
I am a rape survivor
When will the darkness come to
  light?

I worked to overcome this pain
  and shame
I joined groups to talk
To remove the guilt and self-
  blame
I took back the night
I am a rape victor
Or so I pretend
And the darkness surrounds me

I live as half my life never existed
I am selective with whom I share
About how I resisted
About how I fought back
About the pain
About how I was raped
But share I must
Or the darkness will surround and slay me

The questionnaire is before me and I dutifully respond.

Your age at the time of the rape(s)

(Funny how I didn't see the "(s)" before.) The rape I call a "rape" is the one that occurred when I was nineteen. The first date rape was when I was fourteen. The other date rapes happened to me from that time until I was about twenty. Sometimes I was raped. Sometimes I was a willing participant by default. I knew what to expect, so I gave in to the inevitable. Sometimes I was The Victor—I fought off my date-rape assailant.

Your present age *44*

You are female X   male

(Sometimes I've wished I were male. Then I could have the upper hand. Realistically I know that to be a generalization, but I've wished to be able to turn the tables.)

The rapist(s) was (were) known X   unknown X   to you.

If known, indicate relationship

suitors or prospective suitors

(Optional) Did you report the rape to law officials? No X
Yes X

As a fourteen-year-old I didn't know who I was or the importance of my being able to choose my suitors and what we did. It's comforting to write about rape when there is a public forum for that. It's not so comforting for me to talk about my date-rape experiences because I believe they were partly my fault. I know all these situations happened to me because I was not equipped to face life as it was handed to me in my puberty. I also knew no one I could talk to about these things because others believed me to be "nasty."

Sometimes I'm mystified—at nine or ten years of age I had the courage to fight off one of my mother's alcoholic boyfriends who tried to tell me he was doing me a favor by showing me what I shouldn't let little boys do to me. He touched my breasts; I moved his hand with my arm. He touched my stomach where my pubic hair began; I elbowed him and rushed into the house to tell my mother what had happened. She took care of the situation. We left our home for a few weeks, and we never saw him again.

In the next four years, what happened to my knowledge, my strength, my ability to stand my ground? What changed in me over the next seven years to the point where I just let men and boys do whatever they wanted to do to me? I had no real rhyme or reason to the way I allowed them to touch me.

I'd been brought up "right" and morally. Yet, there were times when I would not adhere to these teachings. It seemed that my relationships with boys would start coyly and innocently. Then when my suitor decided he wanted to have sex with me, and if he was successful through date rape, I actually continued the relationship until he never came back.

The turning point in my life, however, was when I returned to Sacramento, where I had lived as a child. I returned as a single parent. My child's father had date-raped me, since I held out in the interest of virtue. We continued the relationship for over two years while we lived in the same city. He did ask me to marry him, but I wanted to know he was marrying me for love, not because he was noble enough to give my baby a name.

In Sacramento, I lived on the "bad" side of town. I reacquainted myself with friends from my old neighborhood. Someone who I wasn't real close to when I was growing up introduced me to a man who was attracted to me. I'm sure they must have had lots of conversations about how they could get the two of us together.

I would talk with him. I even remember going to Fresno with him and my female friend. One thing I knew about him then was that I *never* wanted to be alone with him. Once he said, "Women like to get beat." I thought: I am a woman. I don't like to get beat. I believed that he was crazy to say this, but I was too afraid to say anything to contradict him.

Many months later, my friend and I went over to his house. His mother had gone away for the weekend, so he was home all by himself. My friend (I use the term lightly) and I chatted with him outside near his car. She decided to leave. I didn't have a gracious exit, so when he asked me to come into his house I went.

———

He locked me in, raped me, beat me, and held me hostage from daylight to dark. He would leave the room and admonish me to stay there. Then he'd come back and either beat me or rape me again. I lost consciousness. There was a small window above the narrow bed; however, it was out of my reach. Even by standing on the bed, it was too difficult for me to climb to. Once, he came back into the room as I was trying to make my escape. He pulled me down from the window and beat me again to the point of unconsciousness.

He heard a knock at the door and had me put my clothes on. I came out of his bedroom and perched myself on the edge of a chair that faced the door. An older man and his little boy had come to visit the rapist's mother. The rapist played the gracious host, invited them to sit down, and made polite conversation. I held on to all my belongings. I reached inside my purse, pulled out a birth control pill, slipped it in my mouth, and waited for it to dissolve on my tongue. The rapist stood in front of the open door moving away from it occasionally. The next moment he stood away from the door, I bolted to it and ran two blocks to my friend Jean's house.

Jean had recently divorced. She lived alone with her baby. I pounded on her door. She let me in. I fell in her arms sobbing. Many of those details I don't remember. One thing I do remember is that I took a shower that night. I stood in the shower with the water running over my body, mixing with the tears and sobs that I heaved. I can't remember how long I stayed in the shower. I don't know if the water ran cold. All I remember is that I couldn't get clean enough. I couldn't stop crying.

Jean convinced me I needed to call the police. I was reluctant to do so because earlier in the year I had been gullible enough to believe a man who offered to give me a ride anywhere I wanted to go. He took me to a motel but said that I didn't have to do anything I didn't want to. When he started doing things that made me uncomfortable, I reminded him of his promise to me. He started to beat me. I screamed and fought back until the motel manager came to the bungalow. The police came with flashing lights. I went back to the police station and filed a report. Nothing happened with the case.

This time when I went to the police station, the police said they wouldn't take the report because I'd probably be back with the assailant in the next couple of weeks. Were these people crazy? Evidently, they didn't realize I feared for my life. I didn't go back to my apartment for a long time (I don't remember how long) because he knew where I lived. I didn't know what he had planned for me and I didn't want to find out. I stayed with Jean until I thought I might have worn out my welcome.

I found a clerical position and worked on a temporary assignment during tax season. When they wanted to let me go, I found out there was a vacancy on their staff for a file clerk. I talked the supervisor into hiring me so I could stay off the welfare rolls.

Soon after, my parents came to visit me. My mother noticed the gouge marks on my neck and asked me how I got them. I began to tell her about my rape experiences, thinking that at last I would have someone to sympathize with me. She said, "What were you doing over there anyway?" The words were more stinging than any of the slaps or kicks I had felt from the two other assailants, or the insults of the police.

I stopped talking because I didn't have an answer. I don't know if she started to lecture and scold me. I didn't hear anything she had to say. My dad simply sat silently on the couch. I can't remember anything about the rest of their visit—where they stayed, how long they stayed, if they stayed with me. I just died some that day. But a part of me knew that I had to go on.

I don't ever remember talking about my rape experiences with anyone from that time on. It was just an unfortunate time in my life. I didn't understand any of my feelings. There were no rape support groups. There were no crisis centers. There was only me to figure out how to deal with this, and my way was just to get as far away from it as I could and act like it never happened.

After my parents left, I left Sacramento and attempted a reconciliation with my baby's father. Things didn't work out though, and I joined my parents in their home once more. It was extremely difficult living with them again, and I made my next goal to find a husband so I wouldn't have to support myself alone. I found a job after I'd been there only a short time, but even though I didn't have to pay rent or buy food, I never seemed to make enough money to support myself, much less my son as well. I had my parents' roof over my head and subtle hints that I should find myself a husband.

My first suitor practiced the routine I had come to expect. I said, "No." He said, "But you don't really mean 'no.'" We had sex. I felt guilty and began to cry.

My behavior was definitely not the way I would want it to be written in the Book of Life. I wonder if I will ever be forgiven for my sins? But deep down inside, I know my only sin was wanting to be loved and accepted for who I was. I just didn't know who I was.

When I finally met the man who would become my husband, I presented myself to him as the person I wanted him to think I was—meek, sweet, and obliging. But I had all this repressed history of pain and anger inside me that was wanting to get out.

When we got married he wanted to know about my past, but I didn't want to tell him the whole truth—I had never told anybody the whole truth.

I began to have problems with my job. My performance declined and I even began to weep at work. I felt trapped in my position because I had to answer to an autocratic boss.

I decided to seek psychoanalytic counseling. I remember I told one doctor that I had been raped when I was nineteen. I asked him if that would have any bearing on how I behaved now. He thought for a whole thirty seconds and said, "No." I concluded that session in absentia. My next move was to find a different doctor. I didn't know much about my feelings, but I did know that my being raped did have something to do with a lot of what was going on in my life then.

The doctor I chose next told me honestly that he didn't have a strong background in rape counseling, but he said that he could help me with other issues. I don't feel I got the help I really needed. I wanted a "cure." I think I was there then just to say how terrible life was for an hour every other week. But at least I was talking.

I decided I wanted to go into the field of social services and heard about a sexual assault center where I could get some experience as a volunteer. I called the center's hot line and made arrangements to talk to an advocate. As we talked, I cried. I simply spilled everything. As the words tumbled out, my advocate told me to write about my sexuality or what I would like my current relationship to be like. Being an overachiever, I wrote about both.

This was the first time I had emptied the deep ravine of my life on paper. I had always kept it inside and never really let it out for other people to know about. It was difficult to write about being used by men. It was a relief to be able to review the written word. I felt as I wrote that I had no control over the words on the page as they spewed from my pen. I would remember things and cry. I would remember things and smile. But I kept writing until I had handwritten fifty-one pages.

I gave the advocate my musings to read. I remember she had said that it was refreshing to see that I still had a sense of humor about all this. That was the first time I can remember being validated about my life—being accepted and respected even though I had lived what I thought was such a "dirty" life. This occurred in my late thirties.

I trained to work in the shelter and eventually I worked on the hot line. But there was still a great deal of shame I had not acknowledged. I was still the altruistic crusader. Someone always needed my help more than I needed my help. There was no formal rape group, so I didn't start working on rape issues until much later. I was just glad to know that I was in a supportive environment to nurture the growth I was trying to achieve.

One night, my husband and I happened to be home for the premier episode of "L.A. Law." Three guys were on trial for raping a woman. She looked so much like me. I really identified with her. As she testified from the witness stand, I began to cry.

In the episode, the woman had to defend her honor to the court rather than have the assailants prove they didn't commit the rape. I watched the woman. She was angry. I became very angry. I repressed that anger, probably the same anger I'd been repressing about my own rape experience. I wanted to stop watching the show, but I was unable to move. I kept telling my husband to turn it off, but he wouldn't do it. I cried in a heap on the floor next to him, holding on to his leg. I made it through that emotional hurdle with his support.

About that time, my mother began talking about visiting us, but she kept postponing the trip. One day, she called me with an explanation. She began the telephone conversation with the words, "You know when I was raped . . ." NO! I didn't know she had been raped! I knew a lot of things, but I didn't ever remember her telling me about her being raped! A flood of images came back about stories she had told me. I asked her why she had asked me "What were you doing over there anyway?" when I'd been raped. She said, "That's what they asked me! I didn't know what else to say." Now I understood *everything*, but, dammit, I was angry. Why did she wait so long to tell me?

Throughout my years of marriage and mothering and working, I managed to earn a bachelor's degree. Then I wanted to pursue career goals to become a "success" in the business world. At one point I did find a position that fit with my aspirations, but it was in another city. My husband and I agreed that I should take it. For the first time as an adult, I lived without the responsibility of taking care of someone else. I attended Adult Children of Alcoholics meetings and other similar groups religiously.

I soon discovered, however, that being away from my family was especially difficult when I needed them. One night after watching a television show about rape, I experienced a flashback.

I called my husband miles away. Knowing he was available was wonderful, but it wasn't enough. I cried all night. The next morning I called a crisis center for a therapy appointment, but their waiting list was long. Could I hold on for just a little while? I called the rape crisis center to inquire about support groups. There too the wait was long before a spot would open up. The options available within the community were only helpful if I could suppress my pain for months. I was learning that I could no longer put a lid on it, especially following a flashback. I sought the help of a therapist again until something opened up.

I became involved in a rape victim support group. Each week we told a little more about ourselves. It was wonderful to both support others and to be supported. As I heard about what others had done to help themselves, I set goals for myself. One of them was to speak publicly about my rape experiences at the upcoming Take Back the Night march.

I wrote my speech with much effort. I wanted it to be something I could give to any audience—not solely a group of rape survivors. I asked members of my public speaking club to evaluate it, and one of them agreed to videotape me at the march.

With a lot of anxiety, I marched. Many of my friends and people I had befriended in my Adult Children of Alcoholics group came to support me. When it came time for me to speak, I held my words in a carefully prepared notebook. I read them without a lot of emotion. I believed that if I let out just one emotion, the rest would follow. I wanted to avoid being overwhelmed at all costs.

The power of my words must have been enough. Many people came up to me that night to praise my courage and share their stories with me. Many said that they could not disclose their deep dark secrets, but they appreciated my ability to do so. I had not expected such admiration. I had just considered the speech as a job I had to do.

How has my life changed? I feel like I'm in the position of wondering which came first, the chicken or the egg? Did living in a secretive sheltered household make me vulnerable to victimization? Did my persona greatly change because of my first sexual victimization at nine or ten? Or was it all just fate?

I believe I am a richer person for confronting my past. There's still a little blame and shame, but I'm working on it. I now choose the people I want to share my life with. If they can't accept me as I am, then I don't need them in my life.

My goal is to be an inspirational speaker. If I can achieve that by disclosing the difficulties of my life so others can overcome theirs too, then that I must.

26

The Grace of Sorrow

❧

The first time D. was raped, she was less than two years old. The perpetrator—her father. Then when she was married, her husband raped and beat her; it seems he was simply carrying on his family's tradition. Later in life, three separate times, she was raped by strangers. "I began to feel that society was giving me a message that my body could be taken by anyone at any time. The stranger rapes were the final proof that not only did my father and husband have so-called rights to my body, but any stranger on the street could take me as well." Now thirty-seven years old, D. has told her story to many people. The most common response she receives—"Let's find a reason why this happened to you." One woman told her that she must have been walking "like a victim" before the third stranger rape. In D.'s case, the rapist was so chemically intoxicated that he would not have been able to discern various walking styles. She happened to walk by when he was looking for someone to assault.

In telling her story, D. wants others to know that it is healthy to allow people to experience their pain, especially when the pain encompasses thirty-five years of abuse. "Most people are uncomfortable around pain, and the immediate thing they want to do rather than listen to it is to fix it."

I did not have memories of the incest until after the stranger rapes. After the first two stranger rapes, I experienced a feeling of safety in coming back into the world. But the third time, at gunpoint, I know something broke inside of me. I still do not know if I will recover, and the last time I was raped was thirteen years ago. I am sure that some other people have it worse. I have a friend who works with torture victims from El Salvador. Somehow that knowledge does not help me. In some ways it depresses me more. Something has broken in me and I do not know if I will ever be whole again.

One thing that has been the least helpful to me are pat answers and clichés, especially from New Age people who tell me to live in the present instead of the past. What I really want to say to them is, "Great, can you tell me how to do that? I would be really happy to, but just having a little pat answer is *not* helpful." I have an incredible amount of rage and sorrow that I have never been allowed to express, and that pain lives in my body every day. For someone to come up to me and assume that they have the solution is really an insult.

When I talk about being broken, I feel it in my spirit. I can remember saying as a child and later as a young woman, "This will not crush me and I will stand through this and I will make it." Even with my ex-husband, I remember feeling that my spirit would not be broken by him. By the third time that I was raped, though, I figured, Forget it. You can have my spirit. I obviously have no dignity in this society, so I am not going to pretend anymore. A part of me just gave up. I felt as if there was no point to standing up. If I am constantly going to be knocked down, I might as well just crawl.

My heart was broken as well. I don't trust anyone. I was also abused by my grandmother when I was little, so for me it is not even a matter of trusting men or trusting women. I really don't trust anyone. The pain in my body is pretty constant. It is hard to describe, but it is on both an emotional and physical level. I relive the pain. I feel it in my vagina. The pain in my heart sometimes feels like heat and tightness, and it is difficult for me to breathe.

I have done so many different types of therapy. I have had enough therapy to kill a horse. I have been in therapy groups for sexual abuse survivors. I have done affirmations and I have done rebirthing and I have done Holotropic Breathwork and massage and Rolfing and talk therapy and group therapy. They all may help to a certain extent for an isolated time period, but I do not know if the pain I feel will ever be relieved to any great extent.

I have a lot of anger toward the men who raped me, but in one way I wish they could talk to the men I have been in relationships with. They could say, "This is why D. acts this way. It is my fault. This is what happened to her." I want them to explain it because I am tired of doing it. I know that ultimately I have the responsibility for what I do, but a certain part of my power was taken away. I don't hold my own in a relationship. I am crawling through part of it, and I can not really be a partner to someone if I am on my knees. At times my partners have encouraged me to "take my power." I do not want to get too abstract and blame it on society, but I have to ask, "Where in this society can I take my power?" Sometimes I feel that the only way I can really take some power is with a machine gun.

I cannot count the number of times that I have been accosted on the streets by men telling me to smile: "It is not that bad. Why don't you smile?" I ask myself if feeling like a bliss bunny is the only emotion that is relevant to being a woman. Do men do this to other men? No. They don't. Sometimes I just want to shake men and say, "Excuse me. Give me some respect."

The place that I found to be the most respectful of my feelings was the gay men's community in San Francisco in the late seventies and early eighties. For whatever reason, in that community I felt that I was deemed as whole. I did theater and was really given a lot of free rein to be who I am. Oddly enough, there have been times within the women's community when I did not feel that freedom—I felt restricted. It seemed like I was asked to fit into a certain feminist mold. Ultimately, my time spent there was not empowering. As AIDS became a fact of life in the gay community, I did some volunteer work because I felt like I owed the community a debt of gratitude.

I have found some similarities—I'll just speak for myself—between people living with AIDS and survivors of sexual abuse. I found that with survivors of sexual abuse, myself included, the pain could be so great that you just do not want to live. Sometimes I have felt like I have an invisible disease. Here I am, attractive and healthy, with a nice place to live and an OK job. People say, "What on earth can be so painful that you would not want to live?" To me that is how, yes, the past does control my present. Even after all of these years, I still don't have a great deal of hope that I will come to terms with my past and feel whole again.

Some therapists have encouraged me to find myself by first breaking up with whoever I am seeing. I feel really ripped off by therapy in that way. It seems that they assume any relationship I'm in must be dysfunctional. I feel that the only way I am going to heal with respect to intimate sexual relationships is to keep trying. I do see the value of being alone at certain points, but I also see that one does not get good at something by just thinking about it. I remember one therapist did not see the value of my bringing my partner in with me. She thought that I should just let him go. I had been with this man off and on for ten years—he was my best friend and the person who was there for me through all three stranger rapes. The last time that I was raped, I remember thinking when I got to the door: Things will never be the same. I just felt in that moment that our relationship would never make it through, and it didn't. It was way too big for me. It was way too much for the both of us. Maybe—I can see this in hindsight—if we had had some outside support much earlier on, we would have made it. As it was, just trying to struggle through emotions that big on our own was way too much.

I feel that society wants my pain to be invisible. If I can go and talk to someone with a certificate on the wall and keep it in a nice little neat container for which I pay a huge sum of money, then it is acceptable. Realistically, my pain is not one hour a week—it is all of the time. I don't feel like it is allowed to be real though. If it was cancer, it could be real. Because it is rape and incest, I feel I'm expected to take it somewhere where people don't have to look at it or deal with it.

I did a theater show recently called *Legalize Pain!* One of the things that I talked about was that in our society there isn't really room for people to show their pain. My therapist has wanted me to go on antidepressants. I almost feel like this is one more person who is inconvenienced by my pain.

I also think that what it looks like to be mentally healthy is actually more of what it looks like to be a man in this society. What it looks like to be mentally ill is what it looks like to be a pretty normal woman! "Are relationships important to you? Oh, well, then you are codependent." "Do you express your pain? Then you're hysterical." So what it looks like to be mentally healthy seems to have to do with being independent to a point where needing other people is not really necessary. It just seems to me that this definition of mentally healthy in our society really has to do with not being connected. A lot of women walk around feeling like they are crazy. However, I feel like it is the sense of *dis*connectedness that breeds rapists. My ex-husband was not connected to his feelings. He wasn't free to express his pain to anyone but me, and I was supposed to carry it all. Then he would feel humiliated, so he would want to make me into the sad one, depressed one, the one that had pain. Anger was the only emotion that he felt he was allowed to have and still be a man. Whenever I would show any anger at all toward him, he would beat that out of me and rape me. His mother's response to his beating me was that I was his wife. Her husband had beat her.

One of the ways the rapes have affected me on an everyday basis is that I can be in a movie and will have to walk out if it is too graphic for me. If I sit there and watch it anyway, then I know I am going to be in "nightmare city" for the next few days. The last movie I saw where that happened to me was *The Prince of Tides*. A couple of times I have felt embarrassed, handicapped even, that I could not sit through these things. I get so sensitive at times—commercials come on and I have to turn them off because of all of the bodies and things happening to them. Sometimes I feel that our society just sexualizes everything in this disconnected way, and I feel like I would just puke if I opened up my eyes.

I wish that I could have a more positive relationship with sexuality, since it is such a big part of life. I have had little bits and pieces of my life in which I was able to see sex as fun. And I have often used sexuality as a theme in my theater work and had fun with it in what I hope is a connected positive way for me and the audience. Yet, at this point in my life, that seems so alien to me. Sex—fun—what? I don't think so.

Sometimes when I feel craziest, I read *The Courage to Heal*. It is helpful for me to read the examples about what others did to cope. When *Who's Afraid of the Dark?* comes out, I will be able to take it to those close to me and say, "Read this! This is how I was able to cope."

It has been a year and a half since I first gave my story to this book. I believe that finally expressing my great sadness brought me grace and hope.

I am currently in couples counseling with a man who really cares about me. I feel more willing really to be present in a relationship and less desperate about the outcome. Sometimes I just feel happy and light and glad to be here.

In looking back, I realize there are apologies and gratitude to express to those I hurt by acting out of old pain and anger. I am finally learning how to stand, no more crawling, how to say no and slowly how to say yes.

Now, at times, the memories of abuse don't even seem like mine. This is not dissociation; this is the presence of trust and love. This is something! Maybe because I gave up on results and just went ahead and opened and hurt . . . there was grace.

27

A Glimpse of the Hell Journal

❨

For the past twenty-five years, this woman has documented her experiences of rape in what she refers to as her "hell journal." It has served as an outlet for her inner voice, which she describes as consumed by pain, yet strong enough to convince her to leave her second husband after he raped her. At thirty-eight, she had not shared the contents of her journal with anyone. But when her daughter showed her a newspaper article about this book project, she writes, "I knew it was time to reveal at least a part of my hellish experience. I'm doing this as a form of therapy and for my daughters who love me enough to care and push me to be honest with myself. Thanks, Girls."

This is a lot harder than I ever imagined it would be—to be totally honest with myself. For over thirty years I have had to struggle with the fears, nightmares, anger, lack of trust, lack of control and why's of rape. I have questioned myself and condemned myself to the point of utter frustration. I hated myself so much that I attempted suicide on more than one occasion to try to stop the pain. I have since learned to quit hating myself for something I had no power over.

As a little girl, *I had absolutely no control.* I couldn't stop my father, brothers, and stepfather. I do remember trying once—I was beaten into submission. After that, I quit fighting back because it was just easier to tolerate what was happening. In addition to sexual abuse, there was also mental abuse such as telling me that my mother knew about what they were doing to me and approved. I felt hopeless, worthless, and helpless. They left me feeling like I would never have control over any part of myself. And they had me believing that I asked for it, that I wanted it, and that it was normal. God, were they wrong!

I remember crying myself to sleep, night after night, and screaming into my pillow, "Just leave me alone. I don't want it. I don't like it." I also remember asking God, "Why me? How can you let this happen?" I never got an answer. This affected my belief in God for many years.

When you are raped by someone who says he loves you or someone you "love," it's very confusing to figure out what love really is. One of the first hurdles I had to jump was one of self-hate and self-contempt. I grew up thinking that there were two of me—one the world saw and one who hid away because she thought she was bad or ugly. My belief is that I would not have hated myself as much if I had not known these people. If these people loved me, how could they hurt me this way? How could they have left me feeling dirty, used, and cheap, like I was an object or a possession? I'm almost forty years old and I have yet to figure this out. I could never do this to my daughters. Hopefully I have broken the curse in my family.

When I was a sophomore in high school, I had an English teacher who noticed my bruises and knew what was happening in my home. Fortunately, this teacher also realized that I liked to write. I had been writing poetry as a release from my pain and she encouraged me to keep a journal as a place to be honest with myself. From the beginning, I called these thoughts my hell journal because I felt like I was in hell at the time.

When you grow up, you bring fears and insecurities into your relationships, leaving yourself open for more abuse. I married my first husband to escape the sexual abuse at home. What I walked away from I walked into. He did not sexually abuse me, but I was introduced to a world of alcoholism and drug abuse, as well as more physical and mental abuse. At the time, I thought that I was damaged goods, and I figured that I did not deserve any better. I left myself wide open to further abuse. I gave up on myself and my dreams. I still have them. They just always seem to be beyond my grasp.

I now know why. The part of me I hid away years ago, the "little girl" I tried to protect, believed she was not strong enough to make her dreams come true. That little girl and I have been through hell together, but I felt fairly safe as long as I kept her quiet and hidden. Now she doesn't want to hide anymore. She's screaming to be heard, to say the things I never took time to listen to. At this stage in my life, after raising my daughters, I'm finally ready to stop and listen to her. I kept her silent because it was easier than dealing with the pain and anger she wanted to release.

I have always known she was in me. She let me know it in my poetry, in my journal, and in my many letters to my daughters. But in these instances, she presented a very different side. It wasn't the angry side I have known; it was the dreamer and forgiver, my hopeful side. While my exterior has often been tough and scared, my interior contains the little girl who was loving, creative, and strong. It was she who wouldn't let me die. She has taught me to forgive and carry on when I no longer had the courage or the strength to do so. She never gave up on me even though I had.

I was trying to explain these two aspects of my personality to my daughters. They told me to my surprise that they already knew. The part of me that hurts and shuts down and spends a lot of time in bed is what they refer to as my "quiet side." The "happy-go-lucky side," they said, taught them how to love rainbows, roses, and sunsets. Throughout my life, I had hidden away all that was good from everyone except my daughters. They are my saviors for they have taught me to love unconditionally, totally, and honestly.

I'm now going through my second divorce because my husband of ten years raped me. I had thought that he was different from all of the other men in my life. He was someone I believed in, trusted, and respected. He said he loved me, and I believe he did. He took good care of me and my daughters. He gave us stability, security, a home, and a chance for me to become me. But one night after a party, he raped me. The next morning, I sat in the shower and cried. I was terrified that it had happened again. I went to see my lawyer immediately and filed for a divorce.

This man took something from me that no one had taken in a long time—my trust. I had learned to trust people with *his* support, and then he robbed me of it again. In its place he left a void. At first I thought that maybe I did deserve his treatment, but then I *listened to the little girl inside of me!* She told me that people do not have the right to walk all over me. Finally, after so many sexual violations, I had some control and I chose to leave the situation.

I'm not sure why the rape happened, but I have promised myself to never set myself up to be hurt this way again. If I don't open up, I can't be hurt. For now I don't want any relationships that will allow me to be hurt. I just believe in myself and leave it at that.

I have finally learned to take control of my anger as well, by talking about it and by not locking it inside like I did as a child. I may not have been able to stop the rapes, but I damn sure didn't deserve them. My biggest hope is that if I talk loudly enough and long enough, others will hear and try to stop it from happening.

I still do not have control over my nightmares, nightmares in which I am running from or fighting with someone who wants to hurt me. Most of them go back to my childhood. My counselors tell me that they are not unusual considering my experiences. They say that talking about them and not holding them in will get easier with time, and it has. I believe that when I quit hating myself for not being perfect and not living in a perfect world, the nightmares will ease up too. Even now they come and go. My daughters can always tell when they are coming because they say that I get very quiet during the day, but I wake up the house at night.

The pain of being raped never goes away. Like the nightmares, the pain tends to come and go. Just when I believe I have it under control, it comes back to haunt me, leaving me to hurt all over again.

I know that the kindness of my English teacher has had a big impact on my life. Because of her, I wanted to be a teacher. It has not worked out that way even though I have my teaching certificate. But I have found a compromise. Every spring I work as a camp counselor for two hundred emotionally handicapped children. People always ask me why I gravitate toward the kids who are a handful and how I am able to cope with them. I tell them that I understand where these kids are coming from. After talking to them, I find that they too have been used and abused. We become friends and I give them my phone number. They call me when things come up for them.

Last year, I took in one of the girls. Since she has been living with me, I have helped her to get cleaned up. We spend a lot of time talking. She knows it is true when I tell her I know what she is going through. She has stopped doing drugs and is turning into a wonderful person. In a few months she will be graduating from high school.

Eventually I plan to be one of the loudest voices to stand before Congress. I want to fight for the rights of kids who come forward and say that something is not right in their homes. If children who are abused, sexually or otherwise, are not helped at an early age, then they will just encounter more of the same as adults. A couple of people have told me that when I reach that point, the world better watch out.

I am sure that my English teacher never imagined that her one suggestion would lead to my lifetime commitment to document my feelings and observations. I have written every day. A lot of it is things that I have not been able to come forward and tell anybody yet, even my counselors. I don't trust them enough to know that they will understand what I am saying. If I put it in my journal, then I can go back later and read it. It helps me to understand what was going through my head that day.

I now have three big boxes that contain my hell journal. My daughters know about them. They keep journals too. We have a deal so that we don't look at one another's. I have told them that when they are older I will open them up and go through them. I have let them read this story and it took their breath away. They said that someday I will get my own book out.

The one certainty I know is that you can't lock the memory of rape inside. You have to be willing to get past the fears and pick yourself up and keep going. You can't let it stop you.

Through the years, through all the tears, I have lost pieces of myself. Some of them, such as innocence, I will not get back in this lifetime. I'm no longer searching for them, because I know that no amount of tears or prayers will ever bring them back. But maybe someday when I get to heaven, I'll find the pieces I'm missing. Then I can truly become one.

28

Lost Trust

'

Rape is . . . a conscious process of intimidation by which all men keep all women in a state of fear.

Against Our Will
Susan Brownmiller

Like many young women of the fifties, I was very obedient and trusting and left the decisions of my life up to my mother and father—mostly my father. He was a very controlling man who liked to be "king of the hill" and have his children as serfs to do as he bid. He wasn't completely successful with my two sisters and two brothers, but somehow he managed to control me quite well. Even though I was the eldest I was more the scapegoat than the hero.

We were unaware that my father was alcoholic and that the behavior exhibited in our home was typical of a very dysfunctional family. A child presumes that all families are similar to the one in which she or he was raised. Both of my parents were very volatile, thus the house was always in a state of chaos. All five children escaped as often as possible or hid away in our bedrooms.

I read incessantly and had little interest in school or my future. I assumed my future would entail marriage; thus the rest was unnecessary. My mother always spoke of us attending college but never encouraged participation in school. My parents sent my two brothers to prep school for an excellent education and then to Ivy League colleges. One of my sisters paid her own way through nursing school and the other became a flight attendant. Since I had no training after graduating from high school, I did clerical work at a large insurance company near my home. There were many young men (adjusters) and women (clerks and secretaries), so there was much dating among the employees.

He was a twenty-five-year-old underwriter at the company, just out of the navy. I had dated many of the men from that company but was still a virgin when I dated this man. The night he raped me, he took me to a drive-in and we drank beer. I was not then and am not now a good drinker, so the alcohol went immediately to my head. I only remember him telling me not to worry. At the time I was completely ignorant of sex.

I got pregnant that night and was so unaware that I did not even know I was pregnant for four months. When I told him, he asked—no—told me to set up some other man I had dated. He then proceeded to tell everyone in the company and the small town I had lived in for years that I was pregnant and that someone else was responsible. This made a horrible situation even more ghastly for me and for my family. My parents naturally assumed I had slept with him voluntarily. Others assumed I had slept with other men, but I had not. I knew I had not consented to what occurred that night but lacked a name for it. I did know that if he had raped me just six months earlier, he would have been accused of statutory rape. Finally, in the early eighties, I saw the words *date rape* in an Ann Landers column, and things clicked for me. What a relief!

I returned home after having lived in a Catholic home for unwed mothers. He had just married a very sweet young woman who I had known from Catholic high school. She was six months pregnant. Friends approached me to file charges along with two or three other women who he had also raped. I refused. Foolish move!

They took my baby because thirty-six years ago unwed mothers were not considered "fit" to raise children. They gave my baby to a woman as a "gift"—she had worked for Catholic charities. I was never told of any way (welfare, etc.) that I might keep my beautiful baby daughter. My father did say I could keep her as long as I didn't come home. At nineteen I was very young and totally unprepared to take care of myself, never mind a child.

I tell women that I have been raped, and so often they respond that they also have been raped. I'm almost surprised if I do not get that response. What a tragedy. What is happening to our so called civilized society! I also think that there are many more women who repress that horrible time, as there is little compensation in remembering, never mind speaking of it. We still blame the victims for this offense. Society pretends disapproval, but the men who commit such crimes are not condemned.

About seven years after the rape, I again found myself pregnant. This time I chose abortion, a decision I have never regretted. I would have committed suicide before giving up another child. I was still so devastated by the rape, my first pregnancy, the relinquishment of my child, and confusion as to why it had happened to me. I led the life of a lost soul for a number of years. I had been brought up to believe that if I was a good girl only good things would happen to me. Such a sad myth.

I love children and my husband and I eventually adopted a wonderful, precious girl who has been the light of our lives. As fate would have it, my husband was not able to father children. A good percentage of women who surrender children never give birth to another.

I feel that the rape and the events that followed took away a great deal of trust that has never been fully regained. I do not feel that I am really safe, and I am ever vigilant in all aspects of my life. I do have empathy for people who have had their lives derailed, so I feel I have made the rape work for me in a positive way. I am, however, very distrustful of men—thus a positive and a negative.

Today, at the age of fifty-five, I am a feminist working for the rights of women and children. I have done so for more than twenty-five years with the National Organization for Women, the League of Women Voters, pro-choice groups, and numerous others. I have also been a girls' soccer coach and a Scout leader. I have great hopes for our young women. I've known a great many and they are strong and intelligent with excellent characters. They will be great leaders of our country. They, of course, need to feel safe to pursue their goals and to feel that they can trust their environment.

29

Weeds Have Deep Roots

☾

This forty-three-year-old woman writes:

"There are not a lot of pictures of me when I was little. I do have a picture that was taken within a couple of months of my being raped. I have looked at that picture and been horrified that anyone could touch a little girl. It doesn't seem that it could be possible. It makes no sense to me."

The rape was very early. It happened when I was five. I really suppressed it and would remember only bits and pieces until I was forty years old, when it all came back to me. I remember the threats the man made. I remember the knife. I remember the blood. I remember pain. I remember horror. I remember his wife watching. I do not remember the rape itself.

The rapist went out of his way to ruin my relationship with my father. He did not succeed, but he did make it very difficult. He told me he knew for a fact that my father and my brothers wanted to "do this to you too." This made me terrified of my dad. He and my mom had left me with this couple to go Christmas shopping, and my dad had said to do what they told me to do. So I figured that they were all in on it.

It is difficult to separate the effects of rape, especially when it happened so early. I do know that I had been a very outgoing little girl. Then, suddenly, I was a very shy little girl. I was especially shy around men. I remember a female neighbor whose house I loved to visit. I would watch her cook, and she would give me cookies. But the minute her husband came home, I was out of there! I was no fool.

When the rapist exposed his penis he said, "Big girls like this." Being very precocious, I told him, "No they don't." In adolescence I did not want to be a "big girl," so body changes were difficult for me to accept. Things that other girls looked forward to like lipstick and high heels, I didn't want any part of.

When I was about thirteen, I deliberately gained quite a bit of weight. I remember thinking in some kind of twisted adolescent way that if I ate as much as my dad did, I could be like my dad. I never actually wanted to be a man, but I wanted to skip all of the girl stuff. I thought that boys would leave me alone if I wasn't attractive. I weighed one hundred sixty pounds at one point.

I can divide my life into two periods: before I remembered and after I remembered. They are very different periods involving very different ways of dealing with the world.

Before I remembered, I felt there was something horribly wrong deep inside of me—like I had a terrible secret but did not know what it was. When I was in my early thirties, I began therapy and tried to peel away the layers of secrecy. I did not get the right answer, and it was a very difficult period.

Before I remembered, I lived with a great deal of fear. It was not uncommon for me to believe that if I displeased someone, that person would rape me (or have someone do it). I also had a fear of telephone conversations because I could not see what callers were doing with their hands. I know that both of these fears were irrational, but, at the time, I was not aware of the reason for their existence.

One day when I was driving home from work I remembered that I was raped. Nothing triggered the memory other than the fact that I had been searching for some sort of answer. Suddenly, the thought seemed to come out of nowhere: I was raped! I almost drove off the interstate. I went home and climbed into bed. When my husband arrived, I said, "I was raped." He said, "Oh my god, we have to get you to a doctor!" I had to explain that it had not just happened an hour before.

Once the memories came back, I became extremely angry at this man and his wife. I have a theory that one of the reasons why children can't remember is that they do not have a word for rape. The act is unknown. The word is unknown. There is not a label for what happened.

My therapist helped me work through the rape by going over it again and again. I kept remembering more details and then the flashbacks started. They were terrifying—mainly flashbacks about blood, lots of blood. Once, I was sitting in a big chair in my den. I had been reading and was getting ready to go to bed. I looked down on my lap and there was a spot on my jeans. As I watched, the spot kept getting bigger and bigger and redder and redder. Suddenly there was blood and bits of hair and flesh and it was just creeping up the walls. I have no idea how long that lasted. Then, I was behind a door, and I was looking at all of the blood, and I was thinking, I didn't know that I could bleed there. Very, very scary. It was as though I was facing thirty-five years of fear. There it was, all at once, in a few weeks.

I was very fortunate in having a loving, supportive husband. He shared my pain and supported me in the healing process. It was very difficult for him, but he never gave up. Remembering the rape also brought me closer to the rest of my family. I visited them in North Carolina a few months after remembering. When I told my mom, she was horrified. She said that I shouldn't have to go through the experience of telling anyone else. She asked me who I wanted to tell and said that she would take care of telling them. On that trip, she took care of me in ways that she had never done before. My brother took me back to the house where it had happened and walked through it with me and helped me put together some memories. My sisters, my other brother, and my in-laws were all supportive of me.

During this visit, I had settled down emotionally but still had fits of rage. I visited the graves of this man and his wife. The graves were poorly attended, but things were still growing on them. Standing there above their graves, I got extremely angry and pulled out every single plant, with the exception of two aza-lea bushes. Azaleas have deep roots, and I could not get them out.

I told my father what I had done. You have to understand my father: county commissioner, very distinguished, law abiding, always concerned about what the neighbors thought, very loving, very conservative in his private life. He was a marvelous person. I expected him to be very shocked. He looked at me, sat back, shook his head, and said, "You know, weed killer would do the trick on those azaleas. Wal-Mart sells it and you can get a big bottle for about five dollars." So I went to Wal-Mart and bought a big bottle. It was seven dollars and worth every penny. When I got home, my father took me over to the graveyard in his big Chrysler. He kept saying, "You know, vandalizing graves is a felony." The graveyard was down a dirt road. We drove down, I hopped out, poured the weed killer on the azalea bushes, ran back to the car, and he gunned it. We were out of there! It was wonderful.

Before my father died, he made a point of telling me that one of the most important things for him to do was to let me know that he didn't know anything about the rape, that he wouldn't have let it happen, and that he was very angry that it did. That was really wonderful. He died six weeks ago.

At the age of forty, I suddenly had a realization that there was absolutely nothing wrong with me. I was a very rational person having a very rational response to a very irrational act. Since I have remembered, a friend of mine has said that she likes me better. It is difficult to handle that, but I think I know what she means. She said I am less afraid and less self-conscious. I knew that I had changed, so this was confirmation. Now I am a very assertive person—I get angrier and lose my temper more often. I can't say that once the "bad" stuff was gone, all of the "good" stuff rushed in. It was more like taking out the weeds and putting in the flowers. My life is now extraordinarily different. My relationships, even superficial ones, are satisfying in a way they weren't before. I like people better.

One of the effects, I think, of any kind of violence is that it takes a long time to recognize it, to accept it, to remember it. That is a very scary thing. It is scary to remember, to realize, to say, "I have been hurt." Before I remembered, I would read newspaper accounts of horrible things, and they often meant nothing to me. I couldn't feel. It was as if I had been injected with

Novocain. Since I have remembered, there are days when I can't read the paper. I have to skip over all of the crime news. It hurts too much to read it. These things we read about are not meaningless. They are real.

One of the most difficult things for me was realizing that life is truly not fair. We need to accept that things can happen for no reason. Before my father died of cancer, my older sister asked him, "Why does this have to happen to you?" He said, "Why not me?" That really is the only answer. Why of all the women who walk down the street is it this woman and not the next? Of all the children who are left with baby-sitters, why not this one? Better that it didn't happen, but it did.

I once read that one of the misconceptions that cloud our feelings about abuse is that we tend to equate victimization with innocence. I will never forget that sentence. In order to be a victim, I do not have to be innocent—I could have been the rottenest little girl in history and still have been a victim. It was an atrocity. At the same time, I can't claim any sainthood from being a victim. It didn't make me a better or worse person.

That leads to a big issue for me: responsibility. I can't change what happened. I can change what will happen. I can say that this is me; this is the character I have. Now what am I going to do with it? That responsibility is mine. The violence is something I have to deal with if I am going to go on. All of these things come very slowly, but I do not want to stay in a place where I am a victim; *I did not want to stay in a place where I am the person that this man made me.*

I realize that for a lot of different reasons, some people don't get past being a victim. At the same time, they don't get the good things unless they do. The past cannot be undone, so at some point you just have to say, "It's tough. It's hard, but I have to get on with it."

I think that many people underestimate their own power. I am amazed at what people can do. It is surprising to be able to look at yourself and see what you used to be and what you are now. I am very sorry that people are stuck. Yes, there is so much pain associated with it, just pure agony. I don't mean to lower its value or disregard it, but people need to know that they can heal.

30

It's Never Too Late

❮

Even though Larry was raped fifty-four years ago, he is still fairly new to the recovery process. He did not address the impact of rape on his life until after he saw the movie *The Prince of Tides*. It brought back devastating memories, but he now realizes he has been "too long hiding and too short in accepting the situation."

I am a sixty-four-year-old male who was raped by three men when I was ten years old. The rape has left deep emotional scars, insecurity, almost complete distrust in men and an overdependence on women. The foreign object that was used did considerable damage to my rectal area and continues to cause physical problems. The incident was not reported to law officials or to anyone else. My father is from the "old school," is now ninety-seven years old, and I'm sure he still will not talk about the incident. His only comment at the time was, "Forget that this ever happened."

My father found me after the rape and had to take corrective action to prevent me from bleeding to death. We lived more than ninety miles from the nearest hospital, and he did not have the means to travel, nor the money to afford medical treatment. The action he had to take caused further damage to my rectal area.

Nightmares were a severe problem up until just before my marriage. Although since then the nightmares have greatly decreased in frequency, my fear of having them has often kept me awake late into the night or all night long. This fear always takes place after some traumatic incident.

For years I believed that those men were homosexuals, so I had a very strong prejudice against all homosexuals. My discovery of the error in my thinking occurred about four years ago, and now I know that those men's actions were violent and not sexual.

I have always had a great fear of men and never developed any friendly relationships with men outside of my own family. I am not a small man, but I still fear all men. I cannot go into a room where there are only three men. If I am in a room where the number of men changes to three I will immediately seek an exit, sometimes tripping over objects in my haste.

After every bowel movement I must wash myself very thoroughly (for ten minutes).

I often feel very lonely even when I am in a crowd. I also feel insecure.

If I don't know where my wife or daughters are I imagine all kinds of dastardly situations. In some instances, I've called hospitals and police departments during my panic.

I have always felt comfortable around women, but I doubt that I would have ever trusted myself to have a relationship with a woman if I had not met my wife. She was able to put me at ease and allow our love to develop. I was twenty-eight years old when I had my first real date, and that was with her.

I have never been able to watch a movie where personal violence is involved because I worry that I will cry, and that a man should not show such emotions. I find such violence so abhorrent that it makes me emotionally and physically sick.

I have always had a great need for acceptance, praise, and approval, so I have developed into quite a handyman and will offer my assistance to any project, or to repair anything that needs it. My wife says that I volunteer too much and too often and people take advantage of me. That does not bother me.

Until quite recently, nobody (including my wife) except my long-dead grandmother and my father knew the real reason why I am like I am. When my wife threatened separation or a divorce because of my reluctance to participate in social activities, I finally realized I had to tell her the truth. Since then our relationship has rapidly deteriorated; in fact, she now seems to cringe whenever I touch her. This may all be in my mind. When she looks at me, I see disgust in her face. Since my revelation to her, I began going to a psychiatrist in hopes of solving my problems. I do not as yet know if there will ever be any improvement. She refuses to tell me her complaints about me and refused to speak to the psychiatrist so he can better understand and treat me.

I have told my two daughters of my experience. Only one has offered me any sympathy or understanding.

I often apologize for other peoples' transgressions.

I have long wanted to volunteer to help at the rape crisis center, but I do not feel that I could face people who might suspect or know why I have volunteered. I am too ashamed.

I have always tightly controlled my emotions because I did not want to reveal myself. However, since my recent revelation to my wife, I have not hesitated to show the anger and frustration I feel at all types of sexual or personal violence.

These thoughts have come with much deliberation and great reluctance. I don't know if I can ever really live a more secure and happy life, but I have noted some small improvements. My purpose in these revelations is that my information will be of assistance to you.

Appendix

Resources

❧

Self-Defense

A number of the contributors wrote about the benefits of taking a Model Mugging course. For those of you who are not familiar with this type of self-defense and empowerment program, it involves mock assaults by a fully padded "assailant"/instructor in a supportive environment. Team guides and fellow students encourage the "attackee" to fight back through simple techniques that just about anyone can do. The public is often invited to graduations if you would like to see a demonstration before signing up.

One way to locate the program nearest you is to write or call **Model Mugging of San Luis Obispo** and ask for their newsletter, which contains a listing of programs in the United States, Canada, and Switzerland. The address is: P.O. Box 986, San Luis Obispo, CA, 93406. Phone: (805) 995-1224.

Another way is to call **Impact Personal Safety** at (800) 345-KICK. They also can refer you to a program, although their listing may not be as extensive as that of Model Mugging's newsletter.

Other toll-free numbers for specific areas include:
Bay Area Model Mugging/Impact Self Defense at (800) 77-FIGHT.

Resources For Personal Empowerment at (800) 443-KICK, which serves New York and the tri-state area.

KIDPOWER uses similar techniques and incorporates similar philosophies to teach young people to defend themselves. For more information, contact KIDPOWER at: P.O. Box 1212, Santa Cruz, CA, 95061. Phone: (408) 426-4407.

Support Programs and Other Organizations

Colorado Outward Bound School offers the Survivors of Violence Recovery Progam, a three-day wilderness course that combines counseling with rigorous outdoor activities. Participants take part in exercises that include rock climbing, rappelling, and hiking, which often evoke the same feelings of helplessness experienced during a sexual assault. With this program, the participant is able to conquer those feelings by completing the course. For more information, contact the school at: 945 Pennsylvania Street, Denver, CO, 80203-3198. Phone: (303) 837-0880.

The National Coalition Against Sexual Assault (NCASA) was established in 1978 as a network of rape crisis centers, associated agencies, and individuals working toward the elimination of sexual assault through education, public policy advocacy, and coalition building. If you are interested in learning more about this organization, write to them at: NCASA, P.O. Box 21378, Washington, DC, 20009.

The Los Angeles Commission on Assaults Against Women (LACAAW) is a nonprofit, multicultural, community-based organization whose goal is the elimination of violence against women and children. While many of their comprehensive services are limited to helping those in the Los Angeles area, they do provide nationwide service to deaf rape survivors who wish to receive counseling or general information on the phone. Skilled ASL counselors staff the TDD line at (213) 462-8410. For additional information about their other programs, call (213) 462-1281 or write to: 6043 Hollywood Boulevard, Suite 200, Los Angeles, CA, 90028.

The National Organization for Victim Assistance (NOVA) is a private nonprofit organization of victim and witness assistance programs and practitioners, criminal justice agencies and professionals, mental health professionals, researchers, former victims and survivors, and others committed to the recognition and implementation of victims' rights. NOVA is dedicated to four purposes: national advocacy by serving as the voice for victims in state legislatures and Congress; professional development through training and educational services; membership communication and support through a newsletter and annual conference; and direct services for victims of crime by providing twenty-four-hour crisis counseling and follow-up assistance to victims of all types. If you are interested in becoming a member of this organization or if you would like to speak with one of their crisis counselors, call them at (202) 232-6682. Their address is: 1757 Park Road NW, Washington, DC, 20010.

Survivor CONNECTIONS, Inc. is a grass roots activist organization for nonoffending survivors of sexual assault by clergy, family, youth leaders, counselors, etc., and the supporters of these survivors. They offer the unique service of keeping a confidential database of perpetrators reported by their victims used solely to connect survivors of the same perpetrator for mutual support at their request. They also provide telephone advice, a quarterly newsletter, referrals, and more. To find out more, write or phone survivors Frank and Sara Fitzpatrick at: 52 Lyndon Road, Cranston, RI, 02905-1121. Phone: (401) 941-2548. Fax: (401) 941-2335.

National Self-Help Clearinghouse was founded in 1976 to facilitate access to self-help groups and increase the awareness of the importance of mutual support. The clearinghouse encourages and conducts training activities, carries out research activities, addresses professional and public-policy audiences about self-help group activities, publishes manuals and a newletter, and maintains a database to provide referrals to self-help groups and regional clearinghouses. If you would like more information, contact them at: 25 West 43rd Street, Room 620, New York, NY, 10036. Phone: (212) 642-2944.

Merchandise

The Company of Women is a merchandise catalogue put out by the Rockland Family Shelter to benefit victims of rape and domestic violence. It contains products such as self-defense video tapes, personal security alarms, and travel aids, along with artwork, books, and an assortment of fun items. Some products are sold exclusively through the catalogue. Proceeds from each sale directly benefit women and children who are assisted by the rape crisis hotline or shelter. To order a catalogue, call (800) 937-1193.

If you are interested in learning more about rape on an intellectual level, call your local college or university and ask about their women's studies program. Many are now offering classes in men's studies as well. The **National Women's Studies Association (NWSA)** puts out a directory of affiliated programs. Their address: University of Maryland, 7100 Baltimore Avenue, Suite 301, College Park, MD, 20740. Phone: (301) 403-0524.

Recommended Reading

The following books have been recommended by people affiliated with this book. While the subject matter of some may not specifically address rape, their content can be adapted to apply toward recovery.

Brownmiller, Susan. *Against Our Will: Men, Women, and Rape.* New York: Simon & Schuster, 1975.

If you haven't read it recently, try it again. A comprehensive, readable history of rape.

Conroy, Pat. *The Prince of Tides.* Boston: Houghton Mifflin, 1986.

Fiction, yet discusses female and male rape and its impact on one family in very real terms.

Deng, Ming-Dao. *365 Tao: Daily Meditations.* San Francisco: HarperSanFrancisco, 1992.

Recommended with the idea that a few minutes of contemplation each day can contribute to a spiritual awakening.

Dyer, Wayne W. *Real Magic.* New York: HarperCollins Publishers, 1992.

You'll See It When You Believe It. New York: Avon Books, 1990.

Both books are recommended in regard to rape for their message that all humans have the power to create the person they want to be despite what has occurred in their past.

Fairstein, Linda A. *Sexual Violence: Our War Against Rape.* New York: William Morrow and Company, Inc., 1993.

If you have lost all faith in the judicial system or if you believe that one person can't make a difference, Ms. Fairstein's account of her twenty

years as the district attorney for New York City's Sex Crimes Unit will
convince you otherwise.

Faludi, Susan. *Backlash: The Undeclared War Against American Women*. New York: Crown Publishers, Inc., 1991.

Provides an arsenal of perceptive and witty comebacks.

Katz, Judith H. *No Fairy Godmothers, No Magic Wands: The Healing Process After Rape*. R&E Publishers (P.O. Box 2008, Saratoga, CA 95070), 1984.

The personal account of a university professor who was one of the first to publicly disclose her identity and to suggest that there is no easy cure for rape.

Kingston, Maxine Hong. *The Woman Warrior*. New York: Alfred A. Knopf, Inc., 1976.

A moving collection of family stories including "No Name Woman," Ms. Kingston's interpretation of a family secret.

Ledray, Linda. *Recovering from Rape*. New York: Henry Holt, 1986.

One of the few books to contain information about the long-term effects of rape and male rape. Ms. Ledray writes with a compassionate voice.

Lerner, Harriet G. *The Dance of Anger*. New York: Harper & Row Publishers, Inc., 1985.

Especially recommended if you recognize how anger from being raped is affecting your relationships.

Maltz, Wendy. *The Sexual Healing Journey*. New York: Harper Collins Publishers, 1991.

For those who have sexual problems as a result of sexual assault, a practical step-by-step guide for achieving sexual healing.

Millman, Dan. *Way of the Peaceful Warrior: A Book That Changes Lives*. Los Angeles: J.P. Tarcher, Inc., 1980.

If you view your recovery from rape as a journey, the truths and magic of this book will advance you along.

Scherer, Migael. *Still Loved By the Sun. A Rape Survivor's Journal*. New York: Simon & Schuster, 1992.

A story of strength. Ms. Scherer shares her journal entries for the year following her rape.

Steinem, Gloria. *Revolution From Within. A Book of Self-Esteem*. Boston: Little, Brown and Company, 1992.

In terms of rape recovery, a reminder that in spite of the difficulties each of us face, it is our own inner voice which we must learn to trust.

Tesoro, Mary. *Options For Avoiding Assault. A Guide to Assertiveness, Boundaries, & De-Escalation For Violent Confrontation*. SDEN Publications (Box 986, San Luis Obispo, CA 93406), 1994.

Written with the survivor in mind by one of the cofounders of the Model Mugging program, this book offers tools for (re)creating self-empowerment and preventing assault.

Warshaw, Robin; afterword by Mary P. Koss. *I Never Called It Rape: The Ms. Report on Recognizing, Fighting, and Surviving Date and Acquaintance Rape*. New York: Harper & Row, 1988.

Information based on the national survey which found that only 27 percent of the women whose sexual assault met the legal definition of rape thought of themselves as rape victims. Recommended if startling statistics regarding the frequency of rape are not too overwhelming for you to read about.

If you would like to express your support to any of the contributors of this volume, you may write to them in care of:

Cynthia Carosella
P.O. Box 1797
Boulder, CO 80306